No Man's Land

& Other Places

MURIEL BOL

RETHINK PRESS

First published in Great Britain 2015 by Rethink Press
(www.rethinkpress.com)

No Man's Land & Other Places

CONTENTS

Dedicated to Mihnea

FOREWORD

First impressions, though sometimes false, can have a lasting effect. I remember when, at a purely social event, I first met the author of this book. I felt I was in the presence of a sharp intelligence and an enquiring mind. Time has done nothing to alter that crude impression; moreover, it has filled in detail and embellished the portrait.

Over our long relationship I learned more about Muriel Bol, her interesting career in the armed forces and her affinity with the countries of mainland Europe and with the plight of orphans in Romania in particular. It has been an interesting career and an adventurous journey, to say the least.

The word 'adventure' brings many things to mind. A feeling of new departures, of mystery and of great risk. With her background in military intelligence and the armed forces at a time in the twentieth century when all Europe was in motion, the young Muriel Bol set out upon her grand adventures, a series of separate journeys which took her to such exotic places as Lapland, the Yugoslavia of Marshal Tito, and Anatolia.

In these travelogues, which is how we can describe the diary recollections which follow, she tells us what it was to have been close witness to peoples and customs now erased by passing time and the turn and turn about of historical events. This memoire takes us where few are privileged to go in today's world, a place where travel is not about journey, but more often just about getting 'there', wherever 'there' might be. The world we now live in is that of calculated and managed risk, the 'nanny state' and urban surveillance cameras. As our safety becomes evermore the concern of others our sense of true adventure diminishes, and we are arguably less aware of what it is to be alive.

This is not to say that true adventure does not involve an assessment of the risks involved. Despite the seeming naiveté of this young woman setting out to see the world as it was at that time, we have a sense that she is well aware of the pitfalls that surround her and is very capable of looking after herself.

Whether she is relating her experience with untrustworthy hotel managers or interesting travel companions, she puts us right in the exciting moment with her. But it would be very wrong of me to take you further.

David Nutt

INTRODUCTION

By 1951 Muriel Bol was working for the War Office in Whitehall. Earlier that summer she had made the decision to go on a solo trip that would take her into the Arctic Circle and back. Her incentive was that an atomic scientist with British citizenship named Bruno Ponticorvo had defected to the Soviet Union in August 1950; in the middle of a holiday in Italy, he abruptly left Rome for Stockholm with his wife and three sons, without informing friends or relatives. The next day he was helped by Soviet agents to enter the Soviet Union from Finland. His abrupt disappearance caused much concern to many of the western intelligence services, especially those of Britain and the USA who were worried about the escape of atomic secrets to the Soviet Union.

This turn of events piqued Muriel's interest and she decided there and then that she would like to explore some of the Nordic area. Once her plans became known it was suggested that she should try to make her way up to the Soviet border and prise off one of the metal labels fixed to the posts that ran along the frontier line between Lapland and the Soviet Union. The metal label was of a hammer and sickle. Ever one for an adventure, this challenge was enough for her to decide on a definite course of action.

Muriel went about planning for her holiday during her lunch hours at the War Office. The preparation was to prove a challenge in itself. With very little money behind her and no guide books, no travel agents, no internet, no hotels, no flights, and just unmade roads to be travelling on, this was not going to be easy. In addition, two of the countries she was to travel through were still recovering from German occupation. Postwar tourism, though in its infancy, was encouraged, so there were, at least, cheap tickets to be had. An itinerary for the journey would be essential and was to prove painstaking and gradual.

It quickly became apparent that apart from a few trains in the south, postbuses would the best mode of transport for this traveller. So each lunchtime, for a number of days, Muriel went along to the Foreign Office and the Finnish Consulate, and with regularity asked them patiently for the necessary paperwork and the times and durations of the ferries, trains and postbuses for each leg of her proposed trip. She pored over her trusty Bartholomew's map book, scrutinising each city, town and village in turn.

Fortunately for Muriel, one of the army doctors advised her of the absolute necessity to have a large quantity of mosquito repellent in her luggage; as instructed, she acquired several bottles of Dimethyl Phthalate lotion from John Bell & Croydon in Wigmore Street, London. When researched sometime later, it was found that one of its other uses was in solid rocket propellants. However, at the time it was to prove invaluable to her as the mosquitos were indeed large, vicious and persistent.

She carefully packed one small, leather hand-held suitcase for travelling, containing only a blouse, a jersey, a Harris tweed skirt and jacket, leather gloves of course, a thick coat, warm stockings, a simple nightdress, flannel and soap in a container, one pair of brogue shoes, one lipstick, a comb and a toothbrush. Just the necessities. In 1951, luxury and unnecessary paraphernalia were unheard of for the average post-war citizen. However, being dressed neatly and appropriately was essential. She did also acquire a small cheap camera and a large hat with veiling so copious she resorted to tying it around her waist, in an effort to keep the mosquitos at bay. Not a glamorous look but one that she deemed practical. How right she was.

It had been suggested that whilst on the trip she should photograph any bridges she crossed. The occupying Germans had razed many buildings, much infrastructure and all but two of the bridges, in a scorched earth strategy as they retreated from Finland and North Norway at the end of the war. Main roads had been mined and telegraph lines destroyed. So photographs of any new bridges and their locations might prove to be very handy for the Army Intelligence at some point in the future.

And, so her solo adventure began. Upon her return less than three weeks later, and never one to be dressed inappropriately, she arrived back into London looking for all the world as though she had just taken a pleasure trip to the Lake District, rather than someone who had experienced the travel adventures that she had met with. However, the prized pair of reindeer antlers she held stirred commuters' interest as she passed them by.

Back in Whitehall, Muriel was sent to Singapore to work for 18 months. She then returned to England and was sent for officer's training at the British Staff College in Camberley, Surrey. Once again, she caused a stir on the London Underground as she travelled, arriving at the college carrying a suitcase and hockey stick, tennis racquet, squash racquet and, of course, the much admired reindeer antlers. Several weeks later she passed out as a Major. After a course in advanced intelligence at Maresfield, the home of Intelligence, Muriel was sent out to Trieste. A rare accomplishment for a woman.

By the time she undertook the journey to Marshal Tito's Yugoslavia and wrote the second journal, Muriel had been working in counter espionage for two years based out of Trieste. Yugoslavia was on her doorstep and somewhere she and her team regularly worked.

Her final expedition was to the Anatolian Kingdom, which, unbeknownst to her, was perhaps the most dangerous of the three journeys in this book. Muriel recalls that she was completely unprepared for the different cultural environment and only equipped herself with a pair of very stylish sunglasses, one short sleeved sundress more suited to a cocktail party, and not even a hat. On arrival she simply took everything in her stride. But looking back now, she is amazed at herself.

These travelogues are just a small glimpse into the remarkable life of a fascinating and multi-lingual, multi-talented lady who still has an unusual photographic memory and a curiosity to learn, observe and enjoy life to the full, wherever she is and whomever she encounters.

LAPLAND 1951

This diary was kept to give my
mother a picture of my travels.

LAPLAND 1951

ONE

To Oslo

At 9am Saturday 21st July 1951, I caught the boat-train from King's Cross, and steamed slowly northwards to Newcastle. It was extremely hot, and the countryside of England looked at its best: the poppies blazed in the oats, the hay was cut, and summer reigned. Something was wrong with the engine, so we arrived an hour late at Newcastle, and were hustled through all the formalities that enable we free peoples of the world to leave our birthplace.

A clean and hot second class cabin awaited me on the *Venus* and at 4.30pm, with hooters blowing, we left the grime of Newcastle behind, and sailed towards Norway. The sea was calm and the ship sped through the waters at twenty knots per hour. The next afternoon the lovely coastline of Norway came into view and, as we sailed into Bergen, one felt that at last the holiday had begun.

The weather was still just as hot in Norway, the crowded express from Bergen to Oslo seemed hotter still, and I was the only British person in the carriage. I managed to get a window seat away from the corridor with my back to the engine.

Opposite to me was a Frenchman about thirty years old, dark and good-looking. He spoke excellent English and immediately engaged me in conversation. He explained that he was a doctor on his way to work in a Norwegian hospital some distance north of Oslo. He was amusing and engaging and the eight hour journey passed pleasurably. No one else in the carriage appeared to speak English.

A short time before reaching Oslo, the doctor told me to forget all my crazy ideas of going to Lapland and to come with him: he was in love with me and he wanted me to live with him as his mistress. I shook my head and said, 'No! No! No!'

The train was now nearing Oslo and passengers were moving into the corridor. I went into the corridor and stood looking out of the window. The doctor followed me, insisting that I should go with him: he could not live without me. He was waving his arms about in a demonstrative way and, as he went to catch hold of me, he caught hold of the emergency cord by mistake and the train came to a shuddering halt short of the station.

Everywhere was crowded with people and their luggage, all agitated and shouting that they would miss their onward connections from Oslo. There was nothing I could do. The cord hung limply down beside where I was standing.

I pushed through the people and regained my seat. The doctor followed me. After a while the door suddenly opened and the guard was standing down on the ground looking up at us. Immediately the doctor pointed to me and said, 'She done it, she done it!'

'I did not,' I stated firmly, and explained that the doctor had done it accidentally because he was feeling passionate.

The guard was unmoved, and surveyed us with Scandinavian coldness. Looking at the French doctor he uttered the word, 'Passport,' and beckoned for the doctor to come with him. The Frenchman gathered his luggage and jumped down from the train and was taken off by the guard. After a while the train moved on into Oslo station. No one said anything to me, for which I was grateful.

A school friend of mine named Audrey was married to Jimmy, who worked at the British Embassy in Oslo, running the British Council. They had small children, and Audrey had asked me to make a detour and bring as many tins of blackcurrant purée as I could carry, and a child's scooter that had been left behind.

It was just before midnight, but was not dark, so I went by taxi to Audrey and Jimmy's house and stayed the night.

Next morning I explored Oslo, which I found a dull city, the only remarkable building being the Town Hall, which was huge and very high. It was difficult taking a photograph of it because it was impossible to get far enough away in order to get the top of the building in the picture.

TWO

Journey to Abisko

It was Monday. The fast train northwards left Oslo at 1.45pm in great heat, and first passed through rich wooded country, which changed gradually to mountainous countryside. The train terminated at Trondheim. It was now about 11pm, and I had a sleeping car reserved in the other train (which was waiting), to take me on to Lonsdal, which was as far as the railway went. The weather was still hot, and we left the train at midday on Tuesday, and were crowded into three large buses that were waiting. The bus journey to Narvik took about eleven hours and, after passing through beautiful mountainous country and crossing four fjords by ferry, I arrived in Narvik at midnight.

It was still light enough to read with ease. In fact it was rather like a dull English day. The Royal Hotel was modern, palatial and expensive, but very comfortable and greatly appreciated.

At 10.20am on Wednesday the train left Narvik for Abisko. At the end of the fjord there lay three German battleships whose glorious days had been brought to a sudden and watery end by the British Navy during the Battle of Narvik in 1940. Their rusty sides and bottoms were clearly visible.

At the frontier of Sweden, officials boarded the train and insisted that I should have to get an entry visa because my passport was issued in Singapore. With great difficulty I convinced them that Singapore was not part of India. I then explained what a colony was and how it differed from a dominion. By now there were a number of officials hovering around. They were all very polite, but said I should have to see the police. I next showed them how the Swiss and Norwegians had let me enter without visas, and that I knew there was no need for me to have one to Sweden, that in fact I had enquired in London, and was told it would be unnecessary. I then pointed out the impressive Foreign Office wording on the inside cover of the passport, explaining that Franklin Gimson, Esquire, had been authorised by His Majesty King George VI to issue this passport because the King could not be everywhere at once, otherwise he would have done so himself. This did the trick, and the magic stamp was put on my passport and I was allowed to pass 'freely without let or hindrance'.

I now had my first glimpse of Lapland from the train window. On the right the mountains rose high, with patches of snow lying everywhere. The ground on the left was flatter, where the railway wound along fjords or lakes. But the most striking thing was the rockiness. Rocks were everywhere, even where it was flat; there was hardly any grass, just barrenness. Here and there were a few huts, possibly holiday huts, where fair-haired, brown-skinned families waved as the train went by. The train stopped at various small stations, and finally arrived at Abisko at 12.30pm.

THREE

Abisko

I wandered down a wooded, mossy path towards the lake, making myself realise that at last I was actually in Lapland. There were large, slow-flying mosquitoes everywhere. Their bite does no harm but it is very irritating, especially the way they swarm round, just like flies in England on a summer's day.

I walked down the path, thankful for my insect repellent, and found myself beside a flowing stream. In fact it was a very large one, rushing headlong into the lake, making a great, thunderous noise as the waters fell down the rocks on top of each other, pushing one another out of the way to see who could reach the lake first.

The sun was hot. The path by the lake wound round through low shrub-like trees which were everywhere. The lake was long, and very still and blue with vivid reflections of the snow-capped mountains mirrored in it.

The silence was constantly broken by trains going by, usually goods trains. It seemed a very busy line. All down the banks of the lake were disused dugouts and clearings which could have been gun emplacements.

The wild flowers were numerous: I loved the miniature yellow pansies and large luscious king-cups. So far I had not seen any Lapps or reindeer.

I later discovered that all the land around the lake was the Abisko National Park. I wandered through this and saw some strange little birds and innumerable toads. Strangest of all was the rustling noise just beneath the moss, sometimes beside me but usually just in front and on the left as I walked along. When I stopped to listen, there was silence, and I never discovered what it was.

About 6pm it began to get cool, and I felt in need of a jersey. I climbed up a small mountain, hoping that I might spy reindeer, but I saw none. It was wet underfoot, but hot and sunny, although there were many ominous clouds hanging over most of the distant hills and darkening the lake. On the flat, and half-way up, there were lots of small bushes. I suppose they were really shrubs, but they were all alike and quite harmless, i.e. no thorns, etc.

There were large patches of snow that had fallen deep in crevices and were taking longer to melt. Beside one patch, and almost indiscernible amongst the small broken rocks, stood a dejected bird. It looked like half duck and half partridge. I had not the heart to disturb it, so forlorn and bedraggled it looked, not at all frightened but just intensely unhappy. It was stone grey in colour.

There was not a breath of wind and the mosquitoes swarmed around me in their hundreds. I put on a linen hat, around which was tied yards of white veiling which hung down over my face and shoulders. This baffled most of them but some more adventurous ones came inside. There must have been at least two hundred of them, either sitting on or buzzing around me. They bit through my dress until my shoulders and back were covered with bumps. When I sat down to have lunch the mosquitoes concentrated on my face, and also just below my ankles above my shoes, where I must have missed putting the repellent. I stuffed the food down. By now the inside of my net was also full of mosquitoes. I had to move or go mad.

Down the mountain I ran, following the cairns. It was very wet and four times I went crashing to the ground. Each time the mosquitoes took the opportunity to consolidate.

I did not wish to go back to my hut, but if I was to retain my sanity I knew I should have to. So, hot, footsore, and very wet (from having fallen four times into the water) I returned to my room, thankful for the mosquito netting at the window which kept the room fairly clear.

I washed, changed and lay down. But whenever I closed my eyes, all I could see were thousands of mosquitoes crawling, buzzing, flying and biting: I could not sleep. It was now raining quite fast and was fairly cold. The evening had set in wet and there was no hope of a beautiful sunset.

Next morning was fine, warm and cloudy, in fact rather

oppressive. I went for a walk in the Abisko National Park. It was easy walking among the silver birch trees along well trodden paths beside the River Trask.

There were no roads near Abisko, just the single track railway from Narvik to Boden along which about twenty goods trains a day took loads of ore from Gallivare to Narvik. It was Sweden's greatest export and had priority on the railway. In fact that was the object of building the track.

When the workmen wanted to repair the track they went from place to place riding a tricycle especially made to fit the lines, and when a train came it was quickly removed from the line.

All the engines made many long doleful hoots on their whistles. At first I wondered why, but soon realised that the common thoroughfare was down the centre of the railway line.

The Abisko tourist station was burnt down two years ago and now a new one was being built. Labour was the chief difficulty. There were so few labourers that if they felt like taking days off it was no good sacking them because there were no others. They had to be brought to Abisko with their families and accommodated whilst doing the job. Their quarters were primitive.

The temporary Abisko tourist station consisted of a number of huts. Most of the huts had about six to eight rooms with four bunks in each. There was outside (bucket) sanitation, and only cold water for washing. Most of the hardy people bathed in the stream.

Breakfast was a colossal meal. It began with tomatoes, raw cabbage, cold meat and beetroot with sweet brown bread, butter and cheese. Then porridge swimming in milk and spoonfuls of delicious small sweet, red berry sauce. There was often fried fish and fried potatoes with onions. Always bread and butter with every course; also many glasses of milk. Then bread or rusks with jam and tea or coffee. Most people seemed to have two helpings of everything.

I caught the train that morning to Gallivare. It took about two hours from Abisko and I found myself in the first class sleeping coach. The beds had been changed into seats, and I asked a very round, kindly-looking gentleman, in a uniform covered with gold buttons, if there were any second class seats. He said not in this coach, but since I was only going to Gallivare I could sit in his carriage. I finally decided that he was either a very senior railway customs officer or a police official.

The mountainous country continued for a while, then slowly and surreptitiously changed into rolling hills, and these in turn became smaller with trees growing right to the top. By now there was a smattering of fir trees amongst the birches, and a great deal of water everywhere. Gazing lazily out of the window I suddenly saw a reindeer standing in a clearing.

FOUR

Gallivare

Gallivare is quite a large place, and civilised. On the station there was a very smart looking Lapp in his bright clothes: a dark pleated smock with a border of red and yellow, dark trousers with bright moccasin boots. His crowning glory was the hat: a sort of jockey cap, mostly red, more to one side but practically covering the top. It looked rather as though a red mop had been put on his cap. He was small, dark and appeared active.

On one side of the railway line was a long, reedy, very beautiful lake. On the other side of the railway was the main town of Gallivare. I had lunch at the hotel; an excellent pork chop, and a very nice sweet which tasted like eating raspberry eiderdown.

I wandered through the main streets, of which there were only two. There was a grocer's shop, full of Post Toasties, and a Co-operative Store. The people were smartly dressed, and the small hat shop showed definite style. Most of the cars were Volvos, and also the buses.

I caught the post bus at 5pm to Pajala. The road went through undulating pine forests which stretched to the horizon everywhere. We crossed over seven bridges. The road surface was good and there were no bumps or holes; just a slightly sandy or perhaps gravely surface but where the wheels went the road had been worn smooth.

The bus stopped often, either to deliver post and goods or to collect them. It was full of passengers who had been shopping in Gallivare, and was very comfortable.

Just as we were reaching Tarendo we crossed a wonderful suspension bridge over the River Tarendo. It had been built five years before and was of concrete and steel. A large concrete arch went from bank to bank and the bridge was held up by long steel bars from the arch to the bridge. There was nothing underneath.

Only another forty-five Swedish miles and we arrived in Pajala about 11pm.

FIVE

Pajala

I walked into what looked like an empty hotel. It was a school used as a youth hostel during the holidays. As I reached the door it opened, and a man took my bag and pointed upstairs. The place was gloomy, vast and empty. He took me into a large classroom on the second floor, in which there were four beds: just straw palliasses and straw pillows and one blanket to each bed. The place was empty except for myself, and I was not relishing the idea of being the only inhabitant, when two Norwegian students arrived. They were charming girls and spoke some English.

None of the inhabitants in Pajala spoke English and very few spoke Swedish. They mostly spoke Finnish.

I paid 1 kroen 50 ore for my bed. After having become used to the smell of the straw I slept well but fitfully until almost 10am. I had a very sore throat and could speak only with difficulty. We left the building soon after 10am, and went into the street, I in search of coffee, and they in search of dark brown bread.

To-day was Saturday. I had coffee and some bread, butter and Spam for breakfast, and having bidden *au revoir* to my two delightful bedmates, I now went forth to explore.

The country was flat with pine forests all around. Pajala itself was most depressing. During my breakfast I heard the wireless, tuned into an English programme, with someone singing, 'There's No Place Like Home'. It seemed very strange in Lapland.

Just outside Pajala was a rather fine bridge of concrete and steel. The weather was dull and chilly, which may have accounted for the lack of mosquitoes. I wandered a little way into the pine forest, hoping to come across some antlers, but I only met swarms of mosquitoes, so turned back to Pajala.

Thinking I would have something to eat before going on to Karesuando, I went into a house marked 'Hotel' but found everyone out, so tried another house similarly marked. It appeared that 'Hotel' just meant rooms and not eating, so I was directed to another large house where I managed to get a full Swedish lunch.

Pajala was only a few miles from Finland and all the inhabitants spoke Finnish, and certainly no-one knew any English.

I noticed that they had a small cinema, and the film showing was of a girl who was a prostitute until she saw a sexual psychiatrist, and then she became a happy and normal wife.

The church was the most impressive building. I was informed that it was a Lutheran church. It was white with pale green spire and roof. I could not get in although the notice on the door said 'always open'. There was a strange mark like this on the door:

Apparently religion was nationalised in Sweden and everyone automatically belonged to the State Church. The State paid the clergy, appointed them, and they were responsible for registering all births, deaths, and marriages, etc. I understood that to change from the State religion to anything else was quite a process.

The cemetery was large and wild. Everyone had large family graves, about six times as large as one of our graves. The paths were of gravel and so were the graves. It was obviously not done to have any grass near them. On most graves were granite headstones giving the family name and a cross engraved on it. Sometimes there were a few flowers, but much more common was to plant about six huge silver birch trees on the grave.

I was not sorry to leave Pajala, and I only just caught the post bus back to Muodosombolo at 3.15pm. I did not like the atmosphere inside the bus.

All the way along the route we stopped at little places where I noticed a few posters, two notifying dances, and always at least two others which were communist posters notifying the Peace Meeting in Berlin from 5th to 19th August. Sometimes there was one more which I took to be a local meeting. It seemed that communism had spread across from Kiruna.

Muodosombolo was bleakness itself. I arrived at 8.30pm, and was left standing by the roadside for the bus to Karesuando, coming along in half an hour.

Whilst waiting for the bus I met a young New Zealand scientist. He was also going to Karesuando. He was interesting, and regaled me with stories about the Prague Students Conference, which he had attended the previous year as a representative of the New Zealand students. He was not, and had never been, a Communist. He was now teaching in Stockholm University, and I gathered he worked his passage over as a deck boy. He knew where the youth hostel was in Karesuando, so we stayed there.

SIX

Karesuando

We arrived at Karesuando about 10.45pm. It was cold and misty. We slept in a little red wooden hut, one room for men and one for women. My New Zealand friend left early in the morning for Kiruna, so I bade him *adieu* that night.

Next morning was Sunday. I went out in search of breakfast. It was 10.30am. I went to the Grappes Pensionat and had a huge meal because the next one would not be until 5pm. Here I met a charming girl from the Swedish Broadcasting Service.

She was making recordings with a well-known Swedish lady author who lived in Karesuando, which was a large Lapp centre, especially in the winter. It was also the most northern village and had the most northern church.

I gathered that one hundred years ago there had been terrible drunkenness and violence in Karesuando, which was all changed by a Lutheran priest named Laestadius, and his good work still continued.

The teachers were busy teaching the children Swedish since

they all naturally spoke Finnish. The Finns from nearby were all related to the Swedes, and they shared a common cemetery in Sweden, on an island.

In Karesuando there was a Lapp girls' school. Lapp children had to go to boarding school because of the wanderings of their parents.

Around Karesuando the pine forests finished and the tundra began, with just bushy silver birch trees. The earth was peaty and the grass and wild flowers flourished in the damp.

The cold gets into the tundra and is never really thawed out by the sun. I saw how the cold had made huge crevices between the massive stones of the church, and also between the wood. In places these had been stuffed up with paper and rags. The church was very bare, and the service was in Finnish.

Having walked for two hours along the slowly winding flat road through the tundra, and gazed at the mountains in the distance, which were always blue whether in the morning, afternoon or at night, I returned to the hut to rest.

That evening I had to take the ferry across the water into Finland. The Swedish road ended at Karesuando and the only way northwards was on the Finnish side of the frontier to Kilpisjarvi. There seemed to be no charge for the ferry, which was Swedish.

The rain was pelting down and everywhere was cloaked in mist and dampness. The Finnish frontier post consisted of a tiny wooden hut with all windows and doors always kept shut. The temperature was unbearably hot and was dense with smoke and people. The officials spoke only Finnish and were very slow. I finally emerged and walked some way along a road to join the main road where the bus went to Kilpisjarvi.

SEVEN

Journey to Kilpisjarvi

The bus arrived on time. It was far below Norwegian and Swedish standards, for it rattled, jolted, and made a most extraordinary noise.

This journey was, I think, the most interesting one so far. Apart from a few ageing Finns we stopped at various intervals either to pick up Lapps or to put them down. Whenever the Lapps got in they brought with them a host of mosquitoes and a strong smell of dirt. Perhaps the wet day enhanced the smell, but at times it was almost overpowering.

Their dress and faces were unusual and striking. It was a great temptation to stare. The women were tiny, with very brown skins, high cheek bones and small bright eyes. They looked happy. They wore short dark dresses with rows of bright and different coloured bands stitched to the bottom. Round their necks they wore bright, silk scarves which ended in long tassels and a belt covered with tiny shining trinkets, with a mass of beads and chains around their necks. Their hair was done in two long plaits hanging down, and they always wore a hat, rather after the pattern of the flower monkshood, with brightly embroidered trimmings and white lace around the face. They wore woollen stockings and homemade sabots, or clogs, of leather on their feet.

The men were also tiny, wiry and brown, and rather wrinkled by the weather. They wore smocks, belted at the waist and trimmed with bright coloured bands. They also had brightly embroidered head-dresses, which looked like a kerchief, tied loosely somehow. They wore dark trousers and homemade sabots.

Their children were minute. They were very fair-haired and fair-skinned. They looked pale and pathetic. They wore no shoes nor hats but just trousers and smocks of brown leather, belted at the waist.

We stopped at a Lapp wayside café. It consisted of trunks of birch trees (or pine) put in the shape of a bell tent. Over this were hung sackings, bark of tree or in fact anything until it was all closed in. In the middle was a fire. The smoke, or at least part of it, went out at a hole in the centre; the people sat round on the floor in a circle, drinking coffee and being kippered. The mosquitoes there were the worst I had ever known, being so venomous.

Back in the bus we soon reached the blue mountains I had seen at Karesuando. They were beautiful and just like the Swiss Alps. The road, one made by the Germans during the last war using prisoner labour, was bad, treacherous, and often with a sheer drop on one side. It continued to rain.

Half an hour after midnight we reached Kilpisjarvi. It was wet, misty and very beautiful, tucked away in the midst of the mountains.

Kilpisjarvi consisted of a lake, a youth hostel and various frontier posts. I liked the place, and was sorry not to be staying. At 6am Finnish time, that is 5am Norwegian time, the Norwegian bus left for Tromso. I was only going as far as Nordkjosbotn. It was *still* raining.

We were driven rapidly but most efficiently through the towering mountains, filling up as we went until there was no room left. Everyone was very bright and happy in that early hour and the conductors and drivers were most polite and helpful. All the buses so far arrived and left on time. Very cold and with a streaming cold I arrived at the Gjestestue at Nordkjosbotn at 8.30am.

EIGHT

To Nordkjosbotn

After a glass of milk and a smoked salmon sandwich I went to bed and slept until 2.30pm, when I had *mid-tag*. This was a strange meal of boiled potatoes and something white, tasting vaguely of sausage, swimming in a very pleasant white sauce. Although I still felt hungry, nothing more was forthcoming, so I went for a walk.

The mountains were beautiful: bare and jagged, rising straight up from the sea into the sky. Another also very pleasant thing here was that mosquitoes seemed to be the exception and not the rule. It was a great relief.

The mist came over the tops of the mountains and slowly spread down to the bottom, and was very wet. After half an hour the mist passed and left the most beautiful rainbow I have ever seen. It was just three colours: at the bottom green, then yellow, then flame. After a little while another fainter one appeared some distance higher up. I think it must have been a reflection because the colours were the same, only in reverse.

The rainbow remained for about fifteen minutes before it began to fade.

The grass here was thick and rich, but throughout Norway grass was scarce and therefore precious. Every tiny patch, even right at the waters' edge, was cut for hay, which was dried by hanging it thickly on wires in long rows. The weather was naturally wet and this method was used because they dared not risk losing any of it. When it was dry it was stored in barns.

About a quarter of a mile from here was a magnificent waterfall. The volume of noise caused by the water changed according to the bends in the road. At times it was quite deafening.

The cloud formations over the mountains that morning were fine. The sun was struggling for ascendancy but was having a stiff battle with the clouds and was never victorious for long.

The most common bird around was the magpie (at least I think it was a magpie). They chattered noisily to each other and looked greedy.

Most meals here were exactly the same: an *hors d'oeuvre* plate of cucumber, tomatoes, cheese and smoked salmon, milk, bread and butter and an egg, either fried or boiled.

NINE

To Sørkjos & Alta

The wind was now blowing hard and fresh from the sea. At
4.20pm the bus left Nordkjosbotn and I then discovered that it
did not go as far as Lakselv that day, but only as far as Sørkjos.
We arrived there at about 9pm. During the journey it rained,
sometimes softly, and at other times fiercely. It was a beautiful
journey, especially after we had crossed the ferry at Lyngen.

The road wound round by the fjords, and the sky looked full
of vengeance. The water was still and on the distant mountains
there were transparent colours here and there as if a rainbow
had been cut into pieces and distributed at random. The road
was in fairly good condition, with a few patches of pot-holes
that needed filling in.

The rain became worse and the sky became darker, the distant
mountains looked black as if they were all belching black smoke,
which hung heavily on their summits, and slid part way down.
The sun had managed to burst through the cloud above this
blackness and a golden reflection lined the bottoms of all the

other clouds, and a few patches of blue, a very vivid blue, blazed down in contrast.

Animals wandered along the road in search of pastures new. We met sheep and cows in many places. The sheep always scampered away, but the cows looked moodily at the bus and only sauntered off at the very last moment.

There were very few dogs about and certainly none roaming loose on the roads. Most of the ponies in northern Sweden and this part of Norway were of the same breed. They were a sturdy pony about the colour of a Jersey cow. They had attractive heads. All cows and most horses who were put loose to graze had bells fixed round their necks to enable them to be found easily.

The rain stopped, but the black clouds remained on and around the black mountains. By this time the sun had sunk considerably and was now shining through below the blackness, bathing the tiny islands and the lower part of the larger mountains in warm sunshine. Altogether this type of beauty has far more depth than a clear sky and a blazing sun. There is something fearful and magnificent in it.

The driver of the bus drove as though he was in a tank. Finally we reached Sørkjos, where the local industry was, not unnaturally, fishing. The hotel was the most comfortable I had been to so far since leaving Narvik.

It was then a perfect evening and I was only sorry that my room did not look down the fjord. My cold was now much worse, and I had to retire to bed.

The next morning was Wednesday, 1st August. I was called at 7am, but promptly went to sleep again, and fortunately awakened at 7.50am, leapt out of bed, and was in the bus having had no breakfast, but having paid the bill, with three minutes to spare. This hotel at Sørkjos was the best one and I was sorry that I did not stay there instead of at Nordkjosbotn.

There was just one shower, otherwise the weather became finer every hour. The fjords we passed now ceased to be jade green like the Lgugstj fjord. This part of Norway made use of the peat, and along the road were stacks of cut peat drying. At various places the repairers were busy either widening the road or spreading stones and soil over it.

About 12.30pm the bus broke down. It was something to do with the coil. First the conductor rode on a bicycle in one direction, and returned forty-five minutes later, having had an unsuccessful journey. Next the driver took the bicycle and rode in the opposite direction, presumably in search of a coil.

A very noticeable thing about the north of Sweden and Norway were the bright colours that the people wore. Red was the most popular with their flaxen-haired children. The men wore the brightest check shirts, and the little boys all wore woollen stockings.

Most of the soldiers in Norway wore British battle dress, and also the Air Force. I did notice quite a number of soldiers dressed in the Swedish grey uniforms. I was told that was because the Norwegians were short of uniforms after the war, and they accepted some Swedish uniforms. Norway was quite a poor country, apparently because they had no great export trade.

The driver finally returned and after a total wait of two hours, the bus was repaired.

The sky had now cleared, and the sun was wonderfully warm when we reached Alta. Alta was beautiful, and the Duke of Westminster had a fishing place there. We stopped for a short time at Kistrand, being the most northern point that I was visiting, and then pressed on, reaching Lakselv on a most perfect evening just after 9pm.

TEN

The Midnight Sun, Lake Lakselv and the River Lax

The high, jagged mountains had now given way to tundra with no really high hills, just miles and miles of rolling peaty ground, covered with springy moss, and sometimes wooded with silver birches. This was the most easy walking country.

Having spent thirteen hours travelling in the bus, I simply had to go for a walk before bed. I followed a grassy lorry track through the woods, then slid down a steep bank to the River Lax, where I found some patient fishermen. I followed the river for about a mile. All along the river steam was rising off it to about twenty feet high, and the air was heavy with dampness.

I wanted to take a photograph of the sky at midnight and because of the dampness thought it better to be higher up. On the other side of the river there was a small mountain and this would be the perfect place. The problem was that there seemed to be no bridges and, as I was contemplating where to swim across, I saw a rowing boat hidden in some bushes with the oars inside.

Looking around I could see no one to ask, so I climbed into the boat and rowed to the other side, tied it to a bush and hoped no one would take it away, or I would be stranded.

Fortunately, I was strong and active. I climbed fast and finally reached the summit and sat drinking in the magical moment, the amazing atmosphere, and its muted beauty. The midnight sun of the northern skies was indescribably magnificent and mystical, and I just drank it in until I was full.

Slowly I went back down the mountain and, much to my relief found the rowing boat where I had left it. I rowed back across the river and tied it up where I had found it.

It was just a fortnight too late for the midsummer's night sun. From the north came long straight pale pink streamers, like many search lights and, from the west a warm, golden glow all along the horizon, and on the bottom of the clouds, making them rose-coloured. It was as light as a normal dull English day, but clear and cold. In the east was the glow of a colder, paler light, just a slightly lemon colour. The horses were grazing, the birds flew restlessly from tree to tree, the dew hung in huge drops everywhere and there were innumerable spiders' webs. Slowly I returned.

On the walk, both going out along the bank of the Lax and returning through the woods, the ground was covered with the charred remains of German buildings, vehicles, stores and equipment. Before withdrawing the Germans had systematically burnt everything. Destroyed dug-outs, trenches, stores and gun emplacements were everywhere. It was like walking along with desolate and unhappy spirits. The woods seemed full of the past and unhappiness.

As I came out of the woods the ground became bare, with many mounds and hollows. Voices seemed to scream at me and I found myself running to get away. But from what, I had no idea. I was weeping and moaning and felt intensely unhappy. I had to run and run, I had to get away, for the misery was overwhelming.

After a while I stopped. The air was cool and clean, the place seemed quiet and tranquil. I sat down and was unable to understand what had affected me so much. I walked slowly back to my hotel.

I must have walked about five miles altogether, but was still not feeling at all tired. I went to my room, which was equipped with hot and cold water. How thankful I was to find the hot water, the first time since Narvik eight days ago.

That evening I met the hotel manager, and asked him about the old German equipment, vehicles, etc I had seen. He explained that these destroyed camps had been Serb prisoner of war camps and that the Germans had treated the Serbs worse than any other prisoners. There had been tremendous atrocities. That must have been what had upset me so much and accounted for the atmosphere in and around the wood that night.

Today was 2nd August, a cloudy, healthy, warm, windy day. Having been rudely awakened by a boy of about nine or ten years old bursting into my room in mistake for his parents' room, I ate a colossal breakfast and went for the most enjoyable walk on the tundra.

The peaty earth was springy and dry, the wind bent the birches and kept the mosquitoes off, and it was a sufficiently balmy wind to go without a coat. There were toadstools of every size and colour everywhere, including a huge leather-coloured one about nine inches across and lots of smaller red ones, and all shapes and colours of puff balls.

At long last I found the shrub which gave the scent to the wind. It smelt of a mixture of rosemary and lemon. It had a white flower and was a shrub with leaves like a rosemary bush.

After lunch, another walk, but it was extremely wet, so I took the opportunity of hot water to return and wash my hair. I then had to go to bed while my clothes and hair dried. This was no hardship, and I slept soundly until supper time.

All boys and a great many men in these northern parts of Norway and Sweden wore tightly fitting caps with a bobble on the top, rather like a tea-cosy.

I met a most interesting man who had been sent by the Norwegian government to explore the rocks around Banak for copper ore. He had discovered some but was having it analysed to find out if there was sufficient copper present to make the excavation worthwhile.

The Norwegian government was most anxious to start some sort of industry in the north to solve the problem of unemployment. Some men had been unemployed for so many years that it was doubtful if they would ever be capable of work. The same man told me that these areas in the north were very communistic, caused through unemployment, and that the Norwegian government was trying to counteract it. However, I did not see the communist posters that were so evident in north Sweden.

Since there was such a shortage of labour in Sweden, one felt that the two countries should get together and solve their problems.

ELEVEN

Karasjok and the Finnish border

At 10am on 3rd August, I left for Karasjok. It rained all the way. The road was in great need of repair and wound along beside innumerable lakes. Soon the scenery changed and the barrenness gave way to small and then larger pines which covered the hills. There were no mountains, just vast stretches of water, wonderful rushes, reindeer moss, birds like grouse, and pine trees.

In Karasjok the mosquitoes reigned supreme again. There was a large Lapp encampment, for practically everyone who lived there was a Lapp. Here they lived in permanent wooden huts, and let their men folk go up the mountains with the herds. There was also a new Lapp boarding school. Each room held four beds. There was hot and cold water, and modern sanitation, large airy classrooms and a large library of the most studious books, many of them in English by well-known British authors. This school was founded by the Lutheran Church with some help from the Lutheran parishes in

America. It was really most modern and would put most of our schools in the shade.

In the school was a Lapp exhibition. All the different winter and summer costumes were shown as well as other ones from different parts of Lapland. There were all the implements on show, such as milking bowls, knives, bags and weaving. In winter they wore clothes made of reindeer fur, when the reindeer is not more than about seven months old. This ensured that the skin was soft. The boots were also of fur. Babies had clothes made from the calf of a reindeer, which was wonderfully soft. Their summer clothes were made from blue material gaily embroidered. The colours varied according to the country in which the Lapps lived. The bride and bridegrooms' costumes were indeed very fine and decorative.

I visited a Lapp tent dwelling made of woven cloth round the tree trunks in the shape of a bell tent, with a very large opening at the top. The fire was built loosely in the middle; there were some reindeer skins on the ground for one to sit on; these also served as beds. They used sheets sewn like an army slipper mosquito net to sleep in at night for protection from the insects. There was also a dog. It was a very pale cream colour, with the build of a minute Alsatian. It had yellowish eyes and whenever anyone came near it barked and displayed all its teeth.

The only hotel was full, so I had to sleep in the Lapp boarding school. It was no hardship, and was in fact far more comfortable than most of my other sleeping quarters had been. There were just a few Lapp girls still living there, who had not joined their parents. Every time I met one, which was usually when performing my ablutions, and they were just in their underclothing, they always curtsied, as a form of politeness. I remembered that they had done so in Sweden in Karesuando when they had passed their parson.

By now I had acquired a colossal pair of antlers. They were magnificent but would be a little cumbersome for travelling.

It had rained the whole day and was still raining. I went for a walk through the pines, and nearly jumped out of my skin from artillery fire right beside me. I had unwittingly walked into the Norwegian Army on manoeuvres, practicing their mountain artillery. Quickly and quietly I crept around them, making sure to keep to the rear of the guns. On looking carefully I could see their tents, but they were really very well camouflaged. The mosquitoes were so troublesome that I decided to return.

I then met a very kind and earnest Norwegian girl who had been a social worker and was now training nurses, and one was a Lapp. She was also a member of an international association to do with Moral Re-Armament. She seemed almost shocked that I was quite ignorant of it.

There seemed to be an amount of tree felling just there. The smell of the freshly cut pine was lovely.

From Nordkjosbotn, especially around Lakselv and down here, the Norwegian Army was in prominence. So was the Air Force at Lakselv. I saw a seaplane take off so thought they must have a seaplane base there.

The soil around this part of Norway tended to have only a very thin layer of peat, and underneath was sandy.

'Lapp' is a Swedish word. In Norway they were known as Sami, and Samiski meant Lappish. In Finland it was Lappi.

On awakening on Saturday morning I had a terrible desire to drink gallons of milk. I was not hungry, but just thirsty. I mentioned this desire to the earnest girl and she said that she also wanted milk, so together we went from house to house, from café to café, but no-one had milk. There was so little pasture around Karasjok that the milk had to come from far away and only arrived so many days a week, and not until around 7pm. Finally, in a little, low, green cabin-like café we got two glasses.

On my way back to my room I met three Swedes, whom I had met many times before. They were doing much the same tour that I was doing, only they always arrived just as I was about to depart. They were two brothers and a sister travelling by car. One brother spoke quite good English, and the girl spoke very little but understood more. On hearing that my bus to Karigasniemi did not leave until 7pm, they said that I could go along with them. First, around midday, we had a picnic of coffee and buns in the forest, and then my luggage and I were stowed into the already full car. I did not like to mention that I had some antlers, so discretely left them behind, since there was obviously no room for them.

We soon reached the Norwegian frontier and passed without

difficulty. The Finnish frontier was manned by soldiers. Their uniform was grey, they wore high black boots, breeches, tight fitting tunics done up to the neck, black leather belts and peaked caps rather after the pattern of General de Gaulle's. They were wearing the badge of a bear on their shoulders, and one had various badges going horizontally above his right hand breast pocket and the other had them going vertically. These badges appeared to be for marksmanship and skiing.

The Swedes' passports presented no difficulty but, on seeing mine, the Frontier guard was obviously at a loss, so rang the telephone. There was no reply, so not willing to show his ignorance, he stamped my visa with an air of desperation. Finnish frontier guards did not understand any other language than their own. In fact, generally speaking, I found this so throughout the north of Finland. Some of the guards could speak German, but it was not a popular language.

Immediately after the Finnish frontier the road to Karigasniemi branched off to the right. It was a terribly stony road and much more like a track.

TWELVE

Lake Inari and to Ivalo

We continued straight on to Ivalo. The road from the frontier to Ivalo was quite the best road I had been on so far. It was wide enough for two vehicles to pass at speed, and was in excellent repair. It had a sandy, gravelly surface.

The day was cold, windy and cloudy, but at least the rain kept off. The countryside was just rolling, barren tundra with absolutely no sign of habitation for miles and miles, but just shrubs and rocks covered with reindeer moss.

Reindeer moss was a strange greenish-grey colour. It was dry and sponge-like, and looked about the most unappetising thing growing on the tundra. Nevertheless, the reindeer seemed to enjoy it and ate little else.

By the time we reached Kaamanen, the countryside was flat and the pine forests had begun. There were only four houses there and it looked deserted. Inari was larger but still only a tiny village, with nowhere for tourists to stay. The bridge was not quite complete, so we had to cross on a ferry. The ferries here were hand worked. A wire cable went from bank to bank, and the ferryman and passengers, using huge, heavy blocks of wood with a handle at one end and a groove cut in the other to fit the cable, lever and pull the ferry across. It was hard work and much more difficult than it looked until one got used to it.

From Inari to the town of Ivalo was a beautiful ride, along the banks of Lake Inari through the pine forests. Many reindeer were taken by surprise during their evening stroll.

I arrived at Ivalo about 9.30pm and went to the only hotel. It was large, comfortable, and state controlled. The manageress was delightful and spoke very good English.

Here the new bridge had not been completed and a similar type of ferry to the one in use at Inari was used for traffic whilst pedestrians used a very rickety wooden bridge.

There was a small, plain, wooden church with a red spire surmounted by a white cross. It was new and built by the state. There were no signs of a service on Sunday and the doors were locked.

Just as in the north of Norway, the Germans had carried out their systematic scorched earth policy in Finland, if possible with greater thoroughness.

The new houses were large and substantial and mostly had two storeys. The bank, post office, co-operative stores and a few other shops were huge and tended to dwarf the surrounding buildings.

The postmistress spoke only Finnish and did not know what

stamps should be used for England. In fact, very few English people seemed to stay at Ivalo, but quite a number of Americans and Swiss.

The forests around were state owned, and most of the men worked at timber-felling. Most words here ended in '*i*' such as *hoteli*, *kioski*, *Lappi*, etc. In every little village in Finland, and especially here, there were kioskis: tiny wooden huts where people drank. After the north of Norway and the parts of Sweden I visited, the amount of drinking of beer and spirits here seemed enormous by comparison.

At the back of the hotel and the kioskis, there were always stacks of empty bottles, and on Sunday the kioskis seemed to be constantly full. When I arrived on Saturday night I went into the dining room to have some supper about 9.30pm. The place was full of young men. They had no women with them but were drinking mostly spirits and smoking the Russian type of cigarette, half of which was cardboard.

It was staggering to think how a frontier could make so much difference. The Norwegians and Finns were completely different in all respects. The Swedes I saw near the Finnish frontier had some of the same characteristics, though not in looks.

There was no Scandinavian blondness here, but although some were fair and some brunettes, there were many who were very dark and sallow skinned. Many boys had their hair cropped very short, and there seemed to be little difference in the physique of the young soldier here and the Russian soldier from around Leningrad. In fact they were much more like Russians in all respects.

A most noticeable thing was the men's clothes. They wore poor quality, shiny, off-the-peg suits, mostly of a brown shade, with dirty collarless shirts, and soft light coloured caps. Most of them looked licentious, some much more so than others.

I saw no communist posters but noticed that the films were Soviet exports from Moscow. One was called *Hard Years* and seemed full of violence. The other looked as though it was about Cossacks many years ago.

They had occasional local dances, but I thought that there were many more men than women in this place.

I was the only English person in Ivalo. In fact I was the only intruder; everyone else was Finnish, and I was the only resident in the hotel.

Ivalo was situated where the road from Nantsi in Russia met the road from Norway to Rovaniemi. It was fifty English miles to Nantsi from Ivalo.

Sunday morning my Swedish friends departed, to continue their journey southwards. So I went for a walk northwards along the road we had come the previous day. The day had begun cold and cloudy, but now the sun was blazing hot, the clouds had disappeared as if by magic and the sky was a clear blue. I walked on, kilometre after kilometre. It was a lovely day, the pine forests looked their best, and I rejoiced in the apparent lack of mosquitoes. I then became conscious of gadflies: four of them were buzzing around me trying to attack me from all sides. So long as I kept walking they did not settle, but the moment I stopped, even to take a photograph, they landed, and usually on my legs. I was by now really rather terrified of them, but I discovered that if one could tolerate them the wisest plan was to disregard them completely, as long as they didn't settle where they could sting. After a while, for no accountable reason, they disappeared.

There were signs of a great deal of felling being done, but since it was Sunday, there was no-one anywhere, and the forest was mine for a day. There were still signs of German destruction: German steel helmets in odd places, rubble, rusty parts of vehicles, and a charred forest with millions of blackened tree stumps.

At the eleven kilometre post I saw parts of Inari Lake, so I followed the road along beside the water until the twenty kilometre post. The lake was deep blue, full of lovely rocks and often one single, leafless tree sticking out of the water. To me, it was one of the most lovely spots I visited.

I had left at midday, and by now it was around 5pm. I realised that to be back before sunset I should have to return smartly. I was now conscious of a gigantic blister on my right foot, and a septic toenail (about to come off) on my left foot. I also felt a little hungry and very thirsty (I had left before luncheon). But I was determined not to let anything spoil the day. My whole holiday had been based around Lake Inari and its beauty exceeded my expectations and I was going to devour every moment of it.

Back I plodded. All along the road I met reindeer who were obviously not used to meeting anyone. Once I saw two coming in the distance, so I sat on a rock beside the road, got my camera out, and held it up ready. On they came, right up to me. In fact I thought for a moment that one of them was going to nibble me. Then 'click' went my camera. This startled them, and back they went up the hill, stopping at intervals to look at me.

I met many others, but one in particular seemed to form a sudden attachment for me. He had huge beautiful antlers and we met in the road. He stepped out of my way into the edge of the forest and walked along. Silently we went side by side. Sometimes he was on one side, and sometimes on the other. Then before us was another with even larger antlers. My friend rushed into the road, then back into the forest, then back to the road. This was too much for the stranger. He bolted back the way he had come and disappeared. I had hoped for a moment that I should have seen them fight. My friendly reindeer now disappeared, and I was left to pursue my way alone, except for the gadflies.

No vehicles had passed me, and by 8.30pm I had only four kilometres to go to Ivalo. The sun was just going down behind the tall pines and everywhere had a warm orange glow. The mosquitoes were now everywhere, so I covered my legs, arms, neck and face with insect repellent. Just then a car came along in the opposite direction. It was old and rattled noisily to a stop just in front of me. It was obviously a local car, and on seeing its inmates, I felt a little apprehensive. They were all young men of very scruffy appearance, and two were drunkenly unconscious. The driver was fat and revolting. The back door opened and the young man asked how far it was to Inari. He did not seem at all interested in my reply. Next he enquired in German if I spoke that language. Realising that he was bored with his drunken companions and wanted a little light relief, I replied in English that I did not understand, quietly and firmly shut his door and walked off. He laughed and the car drove on. I strode on even faster to Ivalo and reached there without any other encounters.

I had been walking for nine hours without a rest and had been without food or drink for twelve hours and the day had been hot. I felt exhausted.

The dining room was crowded with people who had arrived by motor coach on an organised excursion. They spoke in Finnish and broken English. I gathered that some were Swedes and Norwegians, and English was the only common tongue.

I drank a jug of milk and had dinner. The milk here was the best I had had. For a salad dressing they used masses of real cream. It was really very good. After dinner I felt sick so went to bed and spent a most restless night.

On Monday morning my feet were still feeling very sorry for themselves, so I spent the morning doing nothing.

I had a most extraordinary and dull pudding for lunch. It was just like not very sweet porridge, but it was brown. I must try and avoid it in future.

After lunch I went for a walk. The sun was brilliant and I wandered along the road to Nantsi. The village of Ivalo straggles down the road and I was gazed upon with interest, being the only stranger in the place. This was a busier road and there were cars and lorries at frequent intervals. After two cars containing young men with short cropped heads who had looked at me in a way I did not like particularly, I took to the forest and walked there keeping parallel to the road. This was a very good, well kept, wide, sandy road. It seemed a very dull road and the forest was difficult to walk in. There were many rocks and thick undergrowth, so I turned back and went to the River Ivalo and sat on the bank and watched the many little boats. It was a fairly wide fast running river, and most of the local inhabitants seemed to use it instead of the road. Very small children managed rowing boats with great dexterity.

All the washing was done in the river. The local hotel had running hot water, but even so all the bed linen was washed in the river. There were special rafts with paths of planks so that the women could walk on the raft and have deep, clean water for washing.

One of the main drinks here was aquavit. Most men's working day clothes seemed to be high black boots and breeches, open necked shirts and caps. It was an almost unseen thing to see a man wearing a tie.

There was only one person here who looked different from the rest. He was about fifty, had a long and unkempt reddish beard, needed a hair cut, wore a dirty, brightly checked shirt and sat silently and alone drinking aquavit. He had a good physique and personality. His face was very bronzed, he was handsome and his features were well bred. His eyes were a very bright blue, truthful and kind. Everything about his face was quite different from any of the other men here. I should have been interested to know his origin.

Dinner here was from 4pm until 7pm. After that one had à-la-carte. I presumed work finished at 4pm. Tonight I had the most wonderful large salmon steak cooked in butter that I had ever eaten.

Toilets in Finland had strange names. For women it was *Naisille* and for men it was *Mehille*. Fortunately they also put a little painting of a man and a woman on their respective doors. In Finland there were no prepositions and *ille* at the end of a word represented 'for'.

Aquavit is a spirit and was drunk neat; it is thirty-eight per cent alcohol and the rest is water. I discovered that the man with the beard was a fisherman from the south. He spent all his time on Lake Inari.

I understood that Russians were never seen at Ivalo. Finnish money had lost its value, and most people were dissatisfied with their wages, and the main topic of conversation was politics. The new Finnish government was a coalition. All Finns seemed proud and interested in the Olympiad being held in Helsinki the following year.

Finnish women worked very hard. They seemed strong but many of them did not look intellectual. Nor did the men for that matter.

I must have eaten something that did not agree with me; I spent an agonising night and had little sleep.

THIRTEEN

To Rovaniemi and crossing the River Kemi

This morning was again sunny and very hot. It was Tuesday, and I decided to move on to Voutso. It was a Lapp village on the way to Rovaniemi. The bus jolted and rattled in a most amazing way. Each seat rattled individually while empty milk churns hurled themselves up and down the gangway. There were many switchbacks, but the driver never slackened his pace. Once or twice I felt certain the bus would leave the road. The seats were hard and cramped. I clutched the back of the seat in front of me to stop my head from hitting the luggage rack when we hit a bump.

We passed through pine forests and bare rounded hills very like the South Downs, then on into the normal Lapp tundra with peaty earth and birch trees. After one and a half hours we reached Voutso.

This was a small village of wooden hut-like houses scattered around. Here the Lapps lived permanently. I believed these were called Scoult Lapps, and were the same as those in Russia, but very different from the Norwegian and Swedish Lapps.

They did not wear the brilliant clothes of those in the north, but were dressed similarly to those at Ivalo, except for some who wear their own home made leather boots.

I went for a walk through the tundra and back through the village. I met a Lapp with some small reindeer antlers, so bought a pair from him for one hundred and fifty marks. On the way back I met a woman doing her washing in a stream. She was strong and brown, with a kind, smiling face. All she wore were trousers and a pinafore. She spoke a little English and, after a long pause, she asked, 'Is England woman all so long?' I hastily explained with signs that English women were all shapes and sizes. I was five feet eight inches tall.

Voutso was at a point where a road not marked on the map went to Lokka. The Russians had taken all the children from Lokka to Russia. One girl of eighteen years had escaped from a political school and managed to get back to her parents in Finland. She was in a very nervous condition.

After an excellent luncheon of omelette, salad and milk, I went for another walk in the opposite direct. But oh! the mosquitoes and gadflies arrived in their thousands and found every tiny spot (especially on my shoulders) where I had not put the Dimethyl Phthalate. In desperation I returned.

The Germans were accused of having first given the Lapps a liking for spirits. But I felt that the Germans were likely to get the blame for everything, even if they were not to blame.

I felt very tired, and went to bed at 7pm. Next morning was

cloudy, but the sun was breaking through in places. I had coffee and a stale bun. The idea of breakfast did not occur to the manageress, cook or waitress, although they knew that I should be travelling until 4.30pm.

The bus arrived from Karigasniemi nearly full with Finns and Norwegians. The road was winding and often up or down hill with lots of switchbacks: in fact most people felt sick. I certainly did.

The road had a top surface of earth, and sand and a hard under surface of well pressed-in stones covered with sand, making a hard and smooth surface where wheels had worn it.

The surrounding country was pine forests to begin with, until after Sodankyte, where there were small farmsteads, and for the first time I saw barley and a few other crops.

Sodankyte was fairly large and was still under reconstruction after the war. There were many large buildings going up and one had the impression that its future would be prosperous.

Finally we reached the Arctic Circle, at least so a notice board stated. The bus stopped and most tourists got out. Straight down the road in the dim distance Rovaniemi nestled in the trees and hills.

To reach Rovaniemi we first had to cross a bridge over the River Kemi. All the bridges north of Rovaniemi had been made of wood; this one was also of wood but the struts were of steel. We then went along on the bank of the Kemi and crossed back across the Kemi by another bridge.

This was a fascinating bridge. The parts in the water holding the bridge up were of huge rocks. As before, the bridge was of wood, the struts of steel, but there was a roof over this bridge, and on the roof was the railway. It really was most economical, and when in a bus, it gave the effect of going through a tunnel with latticed sides.

Rovaniemi must have been the dustiest place in Scandinavia. All the streets and footpaths were made of a loose dusty sand which was blown about whenever there was a wind, and there was wind the day I was there. The dust got everywhere; all over me, also in my shoes, hair and mouth.

I could not occupy my room in the hotel until 6pm, so having an hour to spare, I went for a walk through the dusty streets as far as the railway station. All the shops had shut at 5pm and people were going home. There was a great deal of reconstruction going on and all the new buildings were very similar to all the other new buildings I had seen further north. They were large, plain and white, and they appeared to me very ugly. There was a Lutheran church with a military cemetery, in the middle of which was a large, plain, wooden, white cross and on each grave was a granite block with a name upon it. The roof and spire of the church was of copper and shone in the sunlight.

The hotel was excellent and the food good. I was the only British resident so on my arrival the Union Jack was given a place amongst those flags already hoisted. I had an excellent dinner of pork chop, spinach, etc. The only servant in the hotel who could speak English was the receptionist and I found him a great standby.

I wanted to have a *sauna* (a Finnish bath) and the only time it was available was after dinner. By rights one should eat and drink afterwards. I was told that I should find the bath in the basement, and one went there by using the lift. So at 8.45pm I went into a lift and, seeing four buttons, three of which were marked with numbers, and one that had a mysterious word written in red against it, I took it that the word must mean basement. Accordingly I gave it a hearty press. A loud bell rang through the hotel while the lift remained stationary.

Terrified, I fled back to my room, locked the door and paused. I had had such a job all day trying to make myself understood that I just felt I could not stand a host of Finns attacking me in their unintelligible language, and I felt I should never be able to explain by signs that I had pressed the alarm by mistake for the basement. Creeping out of my room I went to a chambermaid and by signs made her understand that I was looking for the bath. She personally escorted me to a different lift with many buttons and we descended into the basement without further ado.

I went to the bath attendant and was shown into a narrow cubicle where I undressed. Then I went into the next room and had a warm shower and then into a small airtight hot room. Everything in this room was very hot, especially the air. There were three wooden tiers and a platform on the top. On the wooden tiers stood buckets of cold water. In a corner was a huge combustion stove, with what looked like many hot bricks or stones in it. Water was thrown on these bricks and the heat belched forth.

I was told to sit on the top tier and the attendant got a bunch of birch branches, put them on the hot stones, then dipped them in a bucket of cold water and told me to beat myself all over with them. There was no steam, it was just very hot, dry air. The attendant shut the door and left me. After a few seconds I found it unbearable. The air was so hot I felt I could not breathe. Then my eyes burnt so I could not see. Everything went black, so I put cold water from the bucket over my face. That was much better, so with one hand I continued to bathe my eyes with cold water, and with the other hand I clutched the birch brush and feebly beat myself all over.

After five minutes the attendant returned and beckoned for me to come into the next room. Thankfully I left the heat and lay down on a wooden bench which was covered with a sheet. The attendant then soaped me all over twice and I rinsed under the shower. I then had a fairly cool shower and went into an even cooler room.

Here I dried myself and dressed. I had been given to understand that a Finnish bath was most refreshing, but by now I was completely exhausted. I took the lift upstairs and went to bed, feeling wonderfully clean after not having had a bath for two weeks. My room overlooked the River Kemi and I went to sleep to the sound of it rushing by. I awakened at 2.30am, and noticed a star in the sky. That was the first star I had seen in Scandinavia; it was normally too bright for stars at that time of the year. I got out of bed and crawled along the wide window sill, but could see no other stars anywhere. Never before had I ever seen anything so vividly bright as this star. It was large and looked as though it was a chip from the sun. Then clouds floated by and hid it for a moment, then it shone as brightly as before. Then heavier clouds came and hid it completely so I tried to sleep again but could not until 6am.

I awakened at 9am. The sun was brilliant and the day intensely hot. After having paid my bill I had not sufficient marks for breakfast, so I took a taxi to the station and bought a bottle of fizzy drink with the few marks I had left.

FOURTEEN

Journey to Stockholm

The train left at 11.05am. It was small and burnt wood. It had a strange funnel which had a huge bulge near the top and quite dwarfed the train. The coach was very hot and dusty, and only one window in the whole coach was made to open. Then the ticket collector appeared. He was a small, refined, kindly man with a very long humorous face. He seemed intrigued when he discovered that I was English and produced a book in which were written questions in English, Swedish, French, German, Russian, Finnish and Spanish. If there was something I wanted to know I had to point to the question in English. The questions were all numbered and he would look up the same question in Finnish, and he would then somehow give me the answer. He repeatedly told me that the restaurant car was there, and tried desperately to get me to eat and drink at various stations. I did not like to impress on him that I had no Finnish marks, or I am certain that he would have bought me something.

I had to change trains at Kemi and we arrived there at 2pm.

At Kemi the same kind ticket collector produced his son who could speak some English. He was a gentle boy who was a student at Helsinki University, and he was now on his way to Dijon to study French for a month during the university vacation. He had just finished working for a month as a crammer and also a translator in a factory which was how he had managed to afford this trip.

We said *au revoir* to his father, and went on to Tornio. Here we left Finland and after going through customs, etc, we boarded a special train, just for we two, and went over the river to Haparanda, in Sweden. The Finnish trains used a different size track from the Swedish trains.

In Haparanda we hustled through Swedish formalities and boarded the train that was waiting to take us to Boden. In the train my student friend produced a large jar of bottled berries. They looked like large, hard, slightly reddish-yellow raspberries, but their flavour was of strawberries, although they were harder. We ate them out of the jar, he with a knife, and I with a spoon. They were refreshing and I appreciated them greatly, having had nothing all day and it was then 4pm.

Boden was Sweden's Aldershot; full of Army personnel. It was quite a large place and a fairly busy railway junction. Here we changed trains and I had a second-class sleeper reserved. It was a very large train and fortunately had a restaurant car. I had an excellent dinner and felt much better.

The countryside we passed through was forests and lakes and

there was a lovely red sunset glowing through the pines. I went to bed early and slept well until 7am.

On getting out of bed, I was surprised and disappointed to find that it was cloudy and raining hard. We passed through cultivated land and the crops were golden, ready for harvest.

Stockholm was wet and dreary. I plodded off to the Hotel Regina where I had a comfortable room overlooking a delightful inside garden. My respectable clothes had been posted from Oslo, and were waiting for me to collect in their Customs. I walked for about a mile through the wind and rain, collected them and had the dresses pressed.

Gerd telephoned to say that they would collect me at 1.30pm. They then took me around Stockholm by car. The rain had now stopped, but the sky remained cloudy and overcast. I went inside the Palace, visited various old churches and saw Stockholm generally. That evening I was entertained to dinner by Gerd and her brother at the Grand Hotel, which was the Ritz of Stockholm.

FIFTEEN

Return to London

The train left Stockholm for Gothenburg at 9.20am. During this journey I noticed that the countryside looked quite similar to parts of England. Much of the crops had been beaten flat by the wind.

At Gothenburg a terrific wind was blowing and a stormy passage was forecast. This turned out to be true, and from 8pm on Saturday until 7.30am Monday I did not move from my bunk, but remained in a semi-coma without either eating or drinking.

Thankfully I felt the ship steady when we reached the Thames Estuary. It was a cold, blowy morning as we passed the coastal batteries in the estuary and arrived at Tilbury about five hours late.

The train left Tilbury at 1.30pm and arrived at St. Pancras Station one hour later.

The sun was shining.

MARSHAL TITO'S
YUGOSLAVIA 1953

MARSHAL TITO'S
YUGOSLAVIA 1953

ONE

From Trieste to Split

The train left Trieste at 6pm and I arrived at the station with two minutes to spare. To my confusion the guard, who had no front teeth and spoke only Italian and German in a strange lispy way, told me that the train did not go to Fiume and insisted that I should wait until 11pm. Having made a great effort to get to the station by 6pm I was determined to get on the train so, regardless of the protestations of the guard, I entered a second-class coach. The train then began to pull out of the station.

As I walked down the coach a man with a stiff leg asked me if I spoke German and then explained that I was all right on that train but I should have to change at Senpetar. Much relieved, I now gave myself up to enjoying my first trip to Yugoslavia.

This friendly man was an Italian who lived out in the country. He said that his leg was damaged by the RAF. He was very cheerful and talkative, but after a short time he left the train.

Immediately the Italian had left me another traveller came

from his compartment into mine. He was Slav from Fiume. He had a long brown, wrinkled face and walked with a limp. He spoke some English. His expression was kind and he was keen to talk. He was well travelled but had never been to England or America.

We reached the frontier between Italy and Yugoslavia and various Yugoslav officials appeared. I could hear them searching the train thoroughly; seats were removed, luggage searched and every dark corner probed into by torchlight. But they only looked at me and left my compartment undisturbed. They did not even ask me to declare my money, nor did they want to look in my baggage, so I continued reading *The Traitors* by Alan Moorhead.

When we reached Senpetar it was dark and, not having a coat, I felt a little chilly. There was a wait of about twenty minutes for the Fiume train. My Yugoslav friend took me to have a cognac. The barmaid was a sweet girl with a terrible gumboil. My friend gave her a lemon. Lemons were a luxury in this part of Yugoslavia and this girl liked lemon in her tea.

We climbed from the ground on to the train that came in on time and, soon after my friend and I had spread our belongings all over the compartment, we were joined by a large, homely Yugoslav woman who said she did not like travelling alone because she was afraid. I asked my friend of what she was afraid. He just laughed.

It was a clear moonlit night and as the train passed through

Fiume towards the station the place was a blaze of light, especially the dockyard where there was still the sound of work. All along the side of the railway there was bomb devastation. This had been done by ourselves and the Americans.

I left the train at Fiume and, having passed through the ticket barrier, my Slav friend met a friend of his. He was a typical Hollywood edition of a communist spy. His face was pale and where he shaved was dark and he kept his eyes down and shaded beneath a trilby hat worn well down on the eyebrows. His eyes were dark and he blinked nervously through rimless spectacles. He wore a dark overcoat.

Just then a man came up and asked in German about catching the boat to Split, whereupon they asked him to take me along with him. Having said 'goodbye' to my Yugoslav friend, the German carried my case and off we set for the boat. It was not far and the night was pleasant.

The German spoke good English. He had been in England before the war and had seen Princess Elizabeth when she was eleven years old, and Princess Margaret when she was eight, and he had 'the picture still before his eyes'. He thought the British fortunate in having such a good Royal Family and he badly wanted to go to the Coronation. He worked in Belgrade in a commercial business and refused to speak a word of Serbo-Croat.

We finally found the right boat and, after some delay, I managed to get a cabin. It was then 11pm and the boat did not sail until 5am. The cabins were comfortable and there were bunks for four people. Just before 5am I was awakened from a deep sleep by the arrival of the occupants of the other three bunks.

The first to arrive was an attractive American student studying foreign affairs in Vienna. Then came an Austrian with her son, aged seven. The child was excited and it was only with difficulty that he was persuaded to sleep.

I was the first to awaken next morning and found it was 9.30am. I dressed and went on deck to find that we were well on our way down the Adriatic Sea and the day was already extremely hot.

The sea was like a mill-pond and very blue. The coast of Yugoslavia was barren and beautiful in the brilliant sunlight. In the foreground were low stony hills and behind rose a mountain range, just white and stony. As we passed along, there were isolated houses in hamlets where the inhabitants must have lived a life of extreme solitude. Now there were islands of varying shapes on the starboard side. These were also barren and stony and usually uninhabited. I lay in a deckchair basking in the sun, alternately gazing at the scenery, or dozing.

The boat was not crowded and the passengers came from Germany, Austria, Switzerland, England, America and Australia.

For luncheon one could have either a large or small meal. The large luncheon cost four hundred dinars and the small one two hundred. At this stage of the journey I chose the small one. It turned out to be a plain, solid meal, consisting of soup, a great slice of meat, cauliflower, cabbage, potatoes, bread and two apples.

Then back in the deckchair for the afternoon until the sun set and it was dinner time. Again I had a small dinner, which was extremely solid, and soon afterwards, about 9.30pm, we arrived in Split.

During the journey from Fiume to Split we made calls at several small towns, Baska, Zadar and Sibenik. The quays were always crowded, mostly with soldiers or sailors or a mixture of both. They all looked young. These little places were picturesque, especially Sibenik which was built on a hill crowned with an ancient fortress. It looked oriental.

TWO

Split

It was dark when we reached Split but the place was a blaze of light and there was noise of great activity. On the quay a stand was being erected and flags were being hung. Marshal Tito was to arrive next day at 4pm from England. The air was balmy and down the main street by the sea were huge palm trees. There was a full moon and Split looked lovely.

I wandered on down the street and finally found the Hotel Belvue. It was a second-class hotel on the sea front. I had a room which looked on to the sea front where an illuminated fountain was playing noisily.

Two fellow passengers from the ship also arrived at the Belvue and they immediately informed me that they were Bavarians and would be delighted to be of any assistance, and suggested that we all had a drink in the hotel. One of these men was elderly, with spectacles, a red face where his eyes, nose and mouth were all together near the centre of his face leaving a wide margin of forehead, cheeks and receding chin. He was a commercial traveller trying to get contracts for German wares, particularly women's. His friend was younger, heavy and dark featured. He was a schoolmaster, teaching German boys French.

Their conversation, much to my horror, was political, and in loud, clear English they attacked me on each side as to why the British had not stepped into Germany in 1936 instead of waiting until 1939. This harangue lasted for twenty-five minutes without any need for me to say a word. When there was silence and it was apparent that I should have to say something, I laughingly told them that I found it interesting to see how seriously they took politics because, in England, we left politics to the politicians and only took cricket seriously.

They were aghast and impressed on me the seriousness of politics, although they realised that the British nation was far more stable and mature than Germany. After another non-stop political attack of considerable length I managed to let them know that, in my opinion, the Germans should manage their own internal affairs and had better stamp out the Nazi element that was springing up, and that it was already past my bedtime. Thankfully I retired.

I awoke at 5am and found the town awake and full of noise and activity. Huge pictures of Tito and four other leading Yugoslav Communists were being hauled into place, bunting was being strung by sailors right along the sea front, and there was a great deal of shouting.

I dressed at about 7am and, after a breakfast of bread, marmalade and coffee, wandered out to explore Split.

The day was already hot and, after I had gone a little way, I noticed among the Yugoslav flags a Union Jack flying at half-mast from a building which must obviously house the British Consulate.

The British Consul, Major Burton, was busy reporting the theft of tools from his car. He was quiet, kind and charming, and arranged for his interpreter to show me Mestrovic's villa and sculptings in the afternoon.

During the morning I looked around the town of Split generally and Diocletian's palace in detail, or rather, what remained to the present day of this once mighty building on the waterfront.

The palace was built by Cajus Aurelius Valerius Diocletianus (235 – 313 A.D.) who became Emperor of the Roman Empire in 284 A.D. and reigned for twenty-one years. In 305 A.D. he became tired of ruling the Roman Empire and decided to retire and end his life growing cauliflowers in the solitude of the palace he had ordered to be built at Split. It had taken ten years to build the palace, which covered about eight acres, using hundreds of slaves under the direction of Greek masons from Asia Minor. It was built of Dalmatian stone from Brac and granite from Egypt. The original palace must have been a magnificent display of oriental splendour and majesty within the shape of a Roman camp reinforced by massive towers.

When Diocletian died, his palace became the property of the

Roman State and in the 7th century the natives of Salona founded a new settlement within the walls of the palace. Soon the palace began to deteriorate and now nothing but the walls, towers, the interior of the mausoleum, the temple, the vestibulum and the three streets that run from the gates to the centre of the palace were left. There were now about 3,500 people living within the palace walls in slum conditions. In one place, a building four floors high had a whole wall missing, and so four floors had only three walls but, even in this precarious state, the people were still living there quite unconcerned by the publicity of their domestic lives.

I was attracted by the mausoleum, where a Roman Catholic service was being held and, since it was Holy Week, the place was well decorated with flowers and was well attended by a continuous stream of people. Its roof is a dome made of thin bricks, very, very high indeed. Between the floor and the dome are two tiers of columns. The top tier is Corinthian, with a very ornate frieze. I wondered for some time how the slaves had managed to build this dome of such even pattern, and what amazed me still more was the light which was suspended on a chain from the centre of the dome and came many feet down into the centre of the mausoleum. Outside the mausoleum was a colonnade of Corinthian columns which joins on to the peristyle which forms the centre of the palace. Here again are arches or Corinthian columns and, guarding the entrance to the Imperial Tomb, is a sphinx brought from Egypt.

I went out of the palace by the Eastern Gate (The Silver Gate) and found myself in the market where there were rows of stalls of cabbages, cauliflowers and lettuces; also pigs, goats, hens, eggs, red peppers, baskets, brushes, and some flowers, mostly stocks.

I walked a little way into the eastern part of Split, where it is mostly residential. The day was now exceedingly hot and I returned via the outside of the northern wall of the palace and saw the gothic chapel of St. Arnerius. Between the road and the northern wall were vast banks of lavender bushes.

The western part of Split is the commercial side and here there were many tiny shops of every description down tiny winding alleys. I returned to the hotel hot and weary and had a solid luncheon.

At 2.30pm Major Burton's interpreter came to take me to a private view of Mestrovic's villa. Her Christian name was Ria. I can't remember her surname as no one ever used it. She was a charming young Yugoslav woman with breeding and poise. Her grandfather was a governor of part of Hungary, and her father was a Colonel in the Royalist Austrian Army. She was married to a Yugoslav peasant who was a promising sculptor. They had two small children called Tihomila and Ilka.

We walked through a very pleasant and tidy part of the town, along a road by the sea. There were trees along either side of the road and it was peaceful. Ria related how she joined the Partisans and how soon even the stoutest boots wore out on the mountains; of her high regard for Brigadier Maclean and of her stay in Trieste with the Partisans when they were all ordered to behave well, especially to the civilians. The only atrocities she saw were among the Yugoslav army which, she said, were too terrible to describe.

She considered that conditions in Yugoslavia had improved since Tito's revolution with the Cominform and that, during the last year, there was very little UDB (Yugoslav Secret Service) activity and people could talk more freely. Ria certainly talked freely. Her husband refused to join the Communist Party and therefore was not given the better jobs, but Tito wanted him to do a job for him and spent one and a half hours discussing it. Her husband liked Tito very much and she considered that if only the government were like Tito all would be well.

We finally reached a high wall covered with a creeper whose leaves were just coming out in bud. In the centre of this wall was a pair of massive brass doors. On the right of the doors was a lodge built into the wall. Beside the door was a long iron bell-pull; Ria tugged at this and after some delay the doors were opened and we were admitted by a handsome young man who was in charge of the villa. He was obviously a great friend of Ria's.

We mounted three wide flights of steps and in the garden before the villa were three sculptings. One was of a charming nude of a young girl and one was of a rather large woman playing a musical instrument. The villa, designed by Mestrovic, was modern and only one storey high. It had columns in the middle, through which we entered. Metrovic had given his villa to the nation and it had been left just as he had lived in it.

I liked his style. It was definite and strong and quite unafraid. Metrovic was born a peasant, but when quite young his talent was realised and he was sent to Vienna to study sculpting. His first wife was a peasant woman but they had no children and later, when he had begun to make a name for himself and was used to a higher standard of living, he married again, this time an educated woman. They had three children, one boy and two girls. One daughter died later when she had her first child. Mestrovic then went to America.

Most of his sculptings were of peasants, which is probably responsible for the generous dimensions of his women, because the peasant women had to work extremely hard and were very strong. There were many religious pieces, especially wood reliefs. There were two enormous figures cut in wood; they were Adam and Eve and were badly cracked.

We went into the workroom where there were many unfinished pieces. I was particularly struck by one mighty stone piece of a man throwing a weight. Some people would find it repulsive, but I liked it. He had portrayed a nude man of huge proportions and great strength, just tensed up to throw the weight. The stone he used must have been difficult to work on because it was rough and contained many small stones. In this room there were also many finished and unfinished works done by Ria's husband. It was apparent that he was Metrovic's pupil, but he lacked the strength and genius that had made his master great.

Just as we had finished looking round this spacious villa we heard the roar of aeroplanes and, on going outside (this villa commanded an excellent view of the sea), we saw that Marshal Tito was sailing into Split, escorted by two Yugoslav naval ships and a flight of the Yugoslav Air Force. The day was hot and the sky and sea were blue. It was a pleasant sight.

We left Mestrovic's villa and returned to the town to see the Marshal's return. Just past Navy Headquarters was a small pier and drawn up beside it were large American cars used by the very senior Yugoslav Navy and Army staffs. We passed these and then passed the Navy Club, where we reached the crowd. Right the way down the seafront was crowded and opposite the main quay was a vast sea of pink faces in the hot afternoon sun. Then Marshal Tito made a speech that was broadcast throughout the town. Ria translated most of it to me and the crowd cheered loudly at intervals and I could sense that the people were delighted with the speech.

Marshal Tito had been received in Buckingham Palace by the Queen where he had tea with her. It was her first experience of a communist leader. In his speech, the Marshal praised Britain and said that there were no differences between the two countries, and that he was bringing good news to the people of Yugoslavia; that his reception in England had passed all his expectations and that he had been greatly impressed and that Britain was a great nation. He thanked the people of Split for their welcome and said that he was deeply moved. He then inspected the crew of one of his escorting ships.

The Marshal stepped on to a launch and slowly came along the waterfront acknowledging the people, who cheered heartily and with enthusiasm. The Marshal looked very well in naval uniform and very happy. A long, young man took my camera and rushed after the launch, taking photographs for me. Everyone was very excited and the people round me picked me up and carried me on their shoulders so that I could get a better view of Marshal Tito.

The launch then took the Marshal along to the small pier by Navy Headquarters, from where he was taken to the Navy Club for the official reception. All the officials, including the British Consul and his wife, had been waiting there since 3pm, but the Marshal did not arrive until 5pm.

We were by then extremely tired and thirsty, and I accepted Ria's invitation to go to her house and drink Turkish coffee. We made our way through the crowd, past the railway station, and on into the eastern part of the town. We were climbing gently all the way and finally reached Ria's home. The house was modern and ugly and she lived on the first floor in a few rooms with her grandmother, mother, father, father-in-law, sister, mother-in-law, niece, her husband and her two children.

Her husband was small and dark, but unfortunately we had no common language; he had been at home all day and I thought that probably he was awaiting inspiration.

We sat in their living room and drank coffee. In the corner of the room was a bed and on the walls were some fascinating old ornate rifles.

I could not stay long because I was dining with the Burtons, so Ria came with me to show me which bus to catch in order that I could return to the hotel to wash and change. While waiting for the bus, we sat on a wall and chatted. Ria said wistfully how she would like to travel and there were so many places she wanted to see. We were then told that the bus was not coming because the driver had gone to welcome the Marshal. No one seemed to be the slightest bit put out about this and everyone quietly went home. Just then, along came Major and Mrs Burton in the official Humber; they were returning from the official reception of the Marshal. So I climbed into the car and washed at the Burtons.

The British Consul and his wife were satisfied with their lot. They lived in a lovely house on the sea and liked Yugoslavia and the Yugoslavs. He was in the Consulate at Sarajevo and had already been in Yugoslavia for four years. Their fervent hope was that the Foreign Office would forget them and leave them in Split for a further ten years.

THREE

From Split to Dubrovnik

I was up at 5am and, accompanied by the two Germans, walked to the quay to board the boat for Dubrovnik, which left at 6am. One of the Germans went back by boat to Fiume, so only the dreary, disgruntled bachelor came with me. He was extremely liverish and during breakfast, of which he ate a vast amount, he continued his political tirade in a loud voice. It was all rather anti-American and, since he was aware that one passenger was an American, I considered it particularly bad taste, besides which, he should have realised that British people do not talk at breakfast. After having told him that he had a jaundiced outlook, I left him and wandered around the ship.

The sea, sky and coast were all pastel shades of blue, green and grey seen through a pink haze. Everything was indefinite and soft and it was not until the sun dispelled the haze that outlines became definite. We passed through the same type of country as before; a rocky, barren coastline, barren islands and lonely houses.

There were no deckchairs on this ship but the captain, a tall, lean and dark man, gave me his chair to sit on in the captain's part of the deck, with a footrest, a rug and binoculars. It was pleasant lying there in the sun.

A young man wearing corduroy trousers spoke to me in bad French. He was a journalist from Belgrade, on the staff of Borba, the official Yugoslav paper. He had been sent to Malta to meet Marshal Tito and to report on the Marshal's homecoming. He was twenty-nine years old, had been a partisan at sixteen, then trained as a lawyer and, finally, became a journalist.

The first port of call was at Hvar, which is on an island. It was most attractive and tidy and looked very old. A marine officer, wearing a red arm band, descended a beautifully designed flight of semi-circular steps and watched the boat unload and reload passengers. There were a few people standing around and quite a few naval ratings who saluted the marine officer on every possible occasion.

When we resumed our way the countryside had changed and there were many trees, possibly olive trees, growing on the mainland. Also, there were patches of ground where the soil had been ploughed and there were some grassy places. As we proceeded, the land became more fertile.

The navigator, an elderly naval officer with a lined and humorous face, spoke quite good English and told me that he had spent six years sailing between England and America. He knew most of the English ports and considered London too expensive for Yugoslavs. He thought the British had two strange habits: one was cutting bread into thick slices and putting butter on it, and the other was sitting all day in a railway carriage and saying nothing. He liked the English, but he preferred American women. He considered them smarter and gayer, although when English women went to France they behaved as if they were French women and were not nearly as cold as they appeared.

I realised that I had not bought a ticket, so I asked the navigator if I could buy one. He was surprised that I had not bought one and asked how I had managed to get on board without. I explained that I had just walked on rather sleepily, so he fetched a huge dictionary and showed me the words 'contraband' and 'seizure'. Then he laughed and assured me that it really didn't matter and in any case I could not get one because they did not sell them on the boat. I should have bought it in Split.

By now we had reached Korcula. It looked delightfully eastern and was overshadowed by a ruined fortress and the place seemed very Turkish to me. I rather thought of getting off and staying there for a day, but decided not to.

We then passed through a very narrow passage between an island and an isthmus and finally reached Dubrovnik about 4pm.

FOUR

Dubrovnik

The ship docked well outside the old part of Dubrovnik, so I decided to take a tram. All the trams had trailers and the trailers had roofs but no walls. So I boarded an already crowded trailer, accompanied by the journalist. The tram only went as far as the old city, so we walked the rest of the way.

The old city of Dubrovnik was quite distinct from the new surrounding town because it was walled in and there was no traffic. It dated back to the 7th century A.D., but it was not until the 12th century that the present walls were built and, during the following years, impressive fortresses were added. The surface of the walled part of the city covered thirty-five acres.

It was in the 7th century that the Goths, Huns and Avars invaded the Balkan Peninsula, and the old Roman population of Dalmatia took refuge in Dalmatian towns. In the hinterland Slav invaders (Croats and Serbs) organised their small tribal states. The oldest mention of the foundation of Dubrovnik is made in a book by Constantine Porphyrogenetos, in the 10th century. The name 'Dubrovnik' is derived from *dubrava*, meaning a wood or grove.

With the decline of Byzantine power over Dalmatian cities, in 1205 Dubrovnik came under Venetian rule and, after the defeat of Venice in 1358, Dubrovnik acknowledged the sovereignty of the Kings of Hungary and Croatia. In 1526, after the battle of Mohacs, Dubrovnik broke away from the defeated Hungaro-Croatian royal house and accepted Turkish protection. On 6th April 1667 there was a dreadful earthquake tremor which destroyed most of the city. When the Turks were defeated in the Danubian plains, Dubrovnik again acknowledged the rule of Leopold of Hapsburg in 1684, though without breaking her links with the Turks. Venice seized the opportunity of the decline of the power of the Turks and expanded her dominion over Dubrovnik, and was finally expelled by the Peace of Karlovac in 1688. In the 19th century Napoleon invaded Dalmatia and, by a decree of Marmont, Napoleon's General, on 13th January 1808 the government of Dubrovnik was dissolved.

The city walls were two kilometres long and they were most impressive; some parts of these walls could be traced back to the 8th century. The western walls were begun in the 10th century, and finished in the 15th century, and it was through the western gate that we entered the city. The old city was much lower than the surrounding town, which was built on a hillside, so immediately we had to descend some steps and just as we entered the old city there was an orange tree with one large orange on it, well out of the reach of the passers by.

We were immediately in the main street which divided the town in two, running straight from one gate to the other. It was exactly the same stretch along which the old sea channel divided the Roman settlement from the Slav one. Around this street, into which narrow and steep streets descend symmetrically from both sides, there were the finest and most interesting buildings of Dubrovnik.

At the other end of this main street we went out through the eastern gate, known as the Gate of Pile. Here there was an old 14th century drawbridge to cross, because there was a moat around the parts of the wall that face the land.

I had noticed a considerable number of churches, and enquired of my journalist friend, who incidentally was carrying my suitcase, what denomination these churches were. He explained that most were Roman Catholic, but some were Orthodox. I asked him which he was but he assured me that he was an atheist because he was a communist. I asked him what was going to happen when he died. He laughed and said no one had asked him that before but that his mother was Orthodox and had told him all about it. I told him he should give it serious thought because you could never be certain of a long life.

By now, we had nearly reached the Excelsior, the best hotel in Dubrovnik. It was on the sea, outside the old city, but with a very good view of it. The hotel was large, spacious, very modern and empty. It had only been open two days this season. The other people staying there were a dull party of Swiss with a Cook's courier.

The receptionist was an elderly, patronising man who spoke perfect English. I insisted on a front room, and hoped that my journalist friend would now leave me. I shook hands, thanked him and said farewell but he wanted to know if we should promenade, but I assured him that I was tired and must bath.

My room was pleasant, rectangular and had a small independent balcony. I sat on the balcony and read *The Traitors* until it was time to wash and change for dinner.

I went down to dinner promptly at 7.30pm. The head waiter had been in the navy and could speak good English; he was very chatty. Halfway through the meal, to my inexpressible annoyance, I was joined by the journalist. He offered me wine, which I refused, being very annoyed that he should take for granted that I should want his company.

After dinner we had coffee in the lounge and he played the piano. He then said that, since it was such a beautiful night, surely we should promenade. I really did not want to go out with him, so I explained that I did not wish to promenade and that, anyway, I had a bad toe. He was not impressed and got rather cross. He said that English women never worked, they spent all day doing nothing. I retorted that since he had never been to England he was not in a position to know, whereas I had been to Yugoslavia and could, therefore, talk about Yugoslav women with authority. He then said that his friend in the visa section in Belgrade had told him that there were no beautiful English women in Belgrade. I told him not to get his information second hand but to look for himself because, to my certain knowledge, there were two beautiful and attractive English women there.

We chatted a little more and, about 10pm I retired to my room, the journalist still protesting that it was too early to sleep.

Next morning I rang the bell and ordered breakfast in bed. It was the usual coffee, bread, butter and marmalade but here the bread was white, but very dry. After breakfast I went straight out to visit Miss Maw, the only British resident of Dubrovnik.

Right at the top of the hill that towered above Dubrovnik was a large cross. I had been told that Miss Maw lived up on this hillside on the outer skirts of the town in the last row of houses, exactly beneath the left arm of the cross. On the way up to her house, I was just about to pass a woman who suddenly turned to me and asked if I was English. She was delighted to see me and said she was a great friend of Miss Maw. She spoke very good English. As we were chatting a car drew up with three army officers inside. The woman suddenly became agitated and said she did not like to see them. I left the woman and climbed up many steps. There were no roads, just steps and lanes that wound on and up. There were some dainty little donkeys, well laden, being driven down. It was wonderful the way they manoeuvred the steps with such confidence. I next met some children and asked them where Miss Maw lived. They understood Russian and were very well mannered. The boy accompanied me to her cottage.

I discovered Miss Maw in a shed at the top of her small garden. She was very occupied making up Easter presents for all the children and old people of Dubrovnik. She had many friends in England and America who sent her parcels of food. Since she received much more than she needed for herself she gave the rest away at festive times.

She was wearing a black dress to the ground, tightly fitted waist and bodice and long tight sleeves; the dress had many vertical tucks and was high at the neck which was trimmed with white lace. She wore a cameo brooch at the neck.

I found it strange meeting an old, small, frail, autocratic English lady in Dubrovnik who dressed, and had exactly the same manner, as so many old ladies in England thirty years ago. She was so essentially English and county after twenty-five years in Yugoslavia.

Miss Maw actually lived in two tiny huts with a completely detached kitchen. The larger hut had two rooms (one bedroom and a living room) and the small hut had just one room (a bedroom). The garden was full and well kept by a gardener. From the garden and the living room there was the most wonderful view of Dubrovnik below and the Adriatic Sea beyond.

The day was hot (in fact, people were bathing although it was only April) and Miss Maw and I sat in the living room while we chatted and she told me how she came to live in Yugoslavia.

After the First World War, the children of Great Britain saved their pennies so that an orphanage could be built for the war orphans of Yugoslavia. When sufficient money had been collected Miss Maw was chosen to go to Yugoslavia and arrange for the design and building of the orphanage to house fifty orphans. It was built at Nis and Miss Maw was in charge of the orphanage, with several British lady helpers (mostly Scottish).

Most of the domestic staff for the Royal Palace came from the orphanage and any tourist who was in need of accommodation was put up there.

When the Second World War started, the number of children soon increased to seventy-five. Soon the Germans were approaching Nis, so they left their orphanage at a few hours' notice, carrying whatever they could, and trekked from village to village until they found a village where seventy-five children could be housed by putting some with each family. The Germans arrived and immediately sent for the British women and threatened to intern them. They, however, insisted that someone had to look after the children and finally they prevailed on the Germans to let them remain with the children and the Germans sent them all to be accommodated in a lunatic asylum. They actually had a part that had been built separately to house a member of the Yugoslav Royal family. However, the children often saw the lunatics and found their antics fascinating and took to copying them.

Even the Germans realised that a lunatic asylum was no place for children, so they sent them to a barracks. Soon after they arrived, the British Air Force bombed the barracks successfully. Fortunately, all the children were in trenches while the raid was on and were quite unhurt. When the Germans pulled out, the children returned to their orphanage. Then the Russians arrived in a very exhausted condition and took over most of the orphanage but did not otherwise interfere with them.

By the end of the war, all the orphans and helpers were back in their orphanage at Nis: not one had been lost. Then the communist government decided that the children belonged to the state and that the orphanage, which was British property, must be handed over to Yugoslavia.

Soon after the First World War, Miss Maw's assistant, Miss Rankin, had a Yugoslav friend who married an Englishman. This friend had a baby boy and, on her death, had asked Miss Rankin to promise to look after the child. The boy's father married again and took no further interest in his son. Miss Rankin brought up the child, but during the Second World War he, being British, had to be carefully hidden from the Germans. Miss Rankin, therefore, bought this little place in Dubrovnik where they lived in obscurity. When the Yugoslavs forced them to leave the orphanage, their hearts were still in Yugoslavia and they felt it to be their home, so they decided to spend the rest of their lives in this place in Dubrovnik. The boy, now grown up, was married to a Yugoslav and worked for the British Consul in Belgrade. Miss Rankin died one month before I visited Dubrovnik and she left the cottage to Miss Maw during her lifetime and then it was to go to the boy she had brought up.

Miss Maw was awarded the OBE for her work and when Mr Anthony Eden visited Dubrovnik recently he had not time to visit her personally, but sent the British Ambassador to her with the Foreign Secretary's greetings. She was definitely an outpost of the British Empire. She was then seventy-six, and one of her orphans, who used to be nursemaid to the Royal Princes, was now her maid. Miss Maw was the most undomesticated person, as Miss Rankin had always seen to that side; she could only just manage to make a cup of coffee. She was extremely independent, interested and energetic. She kept a visitors book, which included King Alexander's signature and, during the summer, a day rarely passed without a visitor. I was asked to sign the book.

I enjoyed my morning there most awfully and was sorry to leave her. After fond farewells I plunged down the steps, through the wall and into the old town of Dubrovnik.

I spent the afternoon and evening looking around the old town. It was interesting. The roads and narrow winding paths were mostly cobbled. I visited the museum, which was small; just a few rooms with Venetian furniture and some old paintings. It was not inspiring.

Just as it was getting dark I returned to the Excelsior Hotel and the old receptionist told me that my friend the journalist had left; he had gone to Titograd, where he was catching an aeroplane to Belgrade. He had left a message to say how sorry he was not to have seen me before he left.

I had dinner in the large empty dining room where this small, dull group of Swiss were also dining. Their guide, the Cook's courier, came up to me and asked in perfect English if I would join them and have a drink in one of the taverns in the town. I accepted the invitation and discovered that the Cook's man was an Australian. He was pleasant and had no trace of an Australian accent. They were an experimental group to discover if it was possible to start tourism.

In the tavern we met two nautical students; they were studying to become captains in the Yugoslav Navy. One left and returned with a further six. We all sat on upturned barrels and the students sang local songs in harmony. They were very nice boys, who drank little but made a great noise. They were typical students and should have been in by 7.30pm, so they kept a weather eye out in case one of their professors came along. They spoke good English, which language they said was compulsory for nautical students. They walked back with us to the hotel.

FIVE

To Kotor

The following day at about 7.30am I just caught the bus to Kotor. The great joy in travelling early was that it was cool, because every day of this trip was simply sweltering.

The journey to Kotor took about five hours and was a little bumpy. The bus went at great speed along the coast road that went through fertile valleys, where stocks were being grown in strips in the fields. There were also fields of strange little shrubs that grew in the oddest fashion. They were black, there were no leaves or buds but just bare, twisted, knotted, short branches that looked just as if a tree had been planted upside down and that these were roots sticking up. They were vines.

The scenery changed constantly from green valleys to coastal mountainous country. We stopped at small villages and at a few large places, including Hercegnovi. At Hercegnovi a few curious locals collected around the bus and, on learning from the other passengers that I was English, one old man came to me and asked where I came from. I told him Trieste, whereupon he produced a refugee identity card signed by Mr Kellett of the Allied Military Government. He seemed proud of this card. Hercegnovi was a picturesque place on the sea and I wished I had time enough to stay there for a few days.

The road to Kotor wound along the Gulf of Kotor and was a beautiful ride. We arrived about noon.

Being at Kotor was very like being at a Norwegian fjord except that the new hotel was, as usual, too large and out of keeping with its surroundings.

This ancient town, known as the gate to Montenegro, was built within the remains of an old wall on the bottom slopes of a mountain and dated from the 7th century.

The atmosphere was nautical and there were landing craft and other small vessels in the Gulf and many naval officers and sailors in the town. I visited the museum, which was really a maritime museum, and showed naval history of Kotor while under the rule of various foreign powers. One interesting story was of a sea battle between the people of Kotor and the Italians (I can't remember the date but it must have been about a century ago) when an Italian ship was sunk and, as it sank slowly, the Italian flag was the last to disappear. Just before it sank one of the sailors of a Kotor ship managed to grasp the flag. It was later torn into small pieces and distributed as souvenirs to the crew. The captain kept the largest part. When this captain died, he bequeathed his captain's uniform, etc., to the museum and also his part of the Italian flag. During subsequent wars this piece of flag, much cherished by the Kotor people, was carefully hidden because the Italians took every opportunity to get it back.

I saw some very old buildings and churches. The cathedral dated back to the 12th century. There were few shops and little in them. Here, for the first time, I felt the atmosphere of want.

The Hotel Salvia (the only hotel) was not in the town but right outside, with a lovely view down the Gulf looking on to the distant mountains. The hotel was having alterations made and was not ready for tourists. There were ladders, wood, whitewash and workmen everywhere, and constant banging.

I seemed to be the first guest of the season to arrive and, after considerable delay, I was given a room with a lovely view looking down the Gulf at the mountains. One might have been in Norway.

During the afternoon numbers of youths and girls arrived; they were part of a youth conference, and were rather noisy.

The manager of this hotel spoke a very few words of German and since I also speak an equally few number we held very limited conversations, the only trouble being that he was so persevering. He was tall, dark, subservient and with Albanian features. Something about him reminded me of an Indian; it was probably his long thin hands and smooth façade. I felt he would quietly and efficiently knife one with the same serene smile on his face. He was attentive, sent me wine and drinks at every meal, pressed me to accompany him into the town for dancing and a little night life and, when I declined to go out on the excuse of being tired, he stayed with me until I retired to bed.

This manager had spent nine years in Tirana, Albania, and he seemed particularly familiar with the unofficial routes across the frontier. He was also manager of the hotel at Buda. He told me that an American student had gone into Albania, although he had no visa. He said that if I wanted to go, it could be arranged. At that time Albania was tightly behind the Iron Curtain. He did not seem so certain about getting out. During the war he had been a major in the Yugoslav Partisan Army as an inspector. It sounded to me like a Q staff officer. He introduced me to his great friend, who was an engineer, but had been a captain in a tank regiment. I did not care for him either. I had the premonition that if I went out with these two I should never come back. For the first time I felt a little nervous and was anxious to get away from Kotor; even one night there seemed too long.

The next day at 3pm I tried to get on the bus that went to Cetinje. It was crowded with locals, but when a young policeman realised that I was English he promised to get me on. A great deal of shouting between everyone followed and finally a kindly middle-aged woman told her husband, Zacharias, to give me his seat and he was to sit on the floor. This he meekly did. I noticed that he was wearing a British Army greatcoat with general service buttons.

The bus was packed full, with people sitting down the gangway, on the platform by the door and all round the driver. We went roaring through Kotor and along the road that led up the mountains. This road was a masterpiece of engineering. It wound back and forth up the side of a mighty mountain. The journey in the crowded bus was hair-raising. The bends were so sharp, the road was so narrow and the precipice below terrifying. However, the whole time the view was wonderful, especially near the top where there was still a considerable amount of snow. In the bus, some people talked, others sang, while some were sick, but they were all cheerful and friendly.

At the top of this mountain the road wound along amidst many snow-clad mountain tops. An armed policeman travelled on the bus, I presumed to protect it from bandits or gypsies. I saw lots of the latter but none of the former. We arrived at Cetinje in the evening. It was in the mountains where the Montenegrin kings lived in a grand palace. Now only the ruins of the palace remained.

SIX

Cetinje

The only hotel, the Grand, was large and gloomy. There was no difficulty in getting a room for the night. It was evening by now and the sun was setting. I decided to go for a walk and see a little of the town before dark.

The streets were dusty and devoid of traffic. The buildings were never usually more than two storeys high, although some were. I followed a road that wound up a hill with the intention of seeing Cetinje from up there. On reaching the top I sat on a rock and watched the sun set over the town. Unfortunately, about six boys followed at a short distance.

I decided to descend by a little path that went steeply down among brambles and boulders, immediately below the road. Just as I was negotiating the most difficult part, the boys hurled rocks and large stones down upon me. The large rocks they just pushed over the side and there is no doubt that it would have been certain death to have had one on the head. The only thing to do was to look up and dodge the large ones and catch the smaller ones (I was wearing thick leather gloves); in this way my legs were torn by brambles and I was in constant danger of spraining my ankle or falling over a boulder. It was frightening and extremely annoying.

A man with a bicycle had followed me up the hill and had sat at a distance from me when I rested to watch the sunset. He watched all these stones being hurled at me and did not stir, although he looked quite young and fit enough to have coped ably. As I went further away the boys used small flint stones that came whistling at me with surprisingly accurate aim. These I managed to catch by walking backwards.

The stones were coming thick and fast and it was tricky walking backwards, down a steep, stony, narrow track. I was beginning to realise that I could not protect myself much longer when I glanced over my shoulder and saw a large, white Orthodox church with domes and a cross at the bottom of the track on the left hand side amongst tall, dark trees. I did not believe what I saw and thought it was a mirage.

I glanced around again, and the church was definitely there with lights coming from within. It seemed like a miracle to me because the boys were getting much nearer and I expected the worst. The flint stones were so accurate and were coming with great force. Thankfully I was wearing a thick woollen coat and skirt.

The boys were now very near. I concentrated on shielding my face, neck and head, then I darted to the church and went in. I was in another world.

The church was small, dark and crowded. It was built in the form of a cross, with no pews and an uneven stone floor. There were no windows open and the air was heavy with incense and made hot by the many candles which were either held or placed in huge candlesticks. I stood by the door and looked around. At the altar stood the patriarch, supported by three priests. He was wearing golden robes and a golden mitre which glittered with jewels. He had a kind, holy face and long white hair and beard. The altar cloth had been made into the image of the crucified Christ. This image was coloured and made using a form of plastic. On the altar was a magnificent cross, a Bible and a small cross lying down. All round the edge of the altar cloth was a garland of flowers, mostly stocks. The priests took it in turn to chant and there was never a silent moment. Their voices were beautiful.

Soon after I arrived a woman came and grabbed me by the arm and took me to the front and stood me beside the altar. I felt very embarrassed, especially since I was quite unfamiliar with the service, had no candle to clasp and was nearly overcome by incense which was often swung three times right beneath my nose. During the service the altar was cleared and the altar cloth was carried by four priests, preceded by the patriarch, three times round the church. It was then replaced and everything put back on it.

Just after the flowers had been put back, a woman went to the altar and removed a bunch of pink stocks and gave them to me.

I made signs as if to put them back but I was made to understand that they were for me. During all the service people prostrated themselves and kept coming to the altar and kissing the image of Christ all over, also the Bible, the Cross and even the flowers, in fact everything. It was really the most demonstrative form of service I have ever seen. I just stood and clutched the flowers for one and half hours. Then the service ended.

A group of girls in their teens clustered round me fingering my clothes and staring. As I drifted towards the door an elderly woman with a refined face and a slim, slightly stooping figure spoke to me in French. She asked me if I were a journalist and invited me to her house to drink tea. She lived at number eight, Marshal Tito's Market Place.

The drawing room was furnished quietly but expensively. All the furniture was large and heavy. This lady lived with her brother and two other ladies. I did not quite make out whether one was her brother's wife or whether they were both her sisters. Her brother was tall and well built and about fifty years old. He had great charm and spoke good and fluent English. He was a surgeon and was in charge of training nurses. A number of his nurses were being sent to England for training, but they had to have an adequate knowledge of English. This was arranged in conjunction with the British Council who had recently sent a representative from Belgrade to test the nurses.

Her brother asked me if I worked in the British Embassy. I

told him I was in the army and he immediately said, 'I know I should not ask, but you are probably in Intelligence'. He had known a colonel who worked in Military Intelligence in the War Office in Whitehall and he used to visit him.

The three women were all beautiful in a 'Madonna' way. Their expressions were composed and serene; their features regular and fine; their hair braided round their heads and their hands folded quietly on their laps. None of them was eating and they drank only water because they were fasting until Easter Sunday.

We chatted about various topics of general interest, particularly about Trieste. They were well educated and cultured and before the war they had travelled. They were very pro-British and were delighted at the psychological change of friendship towards Britain after Marshal Tito's recent visit. After requests to visit them whenever I came to Cetinje, I thanked them and went to my hotel.

There was only one public room, which was already fairly full of men of all ages who were mostly drinking. It reminded me very much of the hotels in northern Finland. I was stared at and great interest was taken in my dinner, which was dull and not very satisfying. After having ensured that I would get an early call at 5am I went to bed.

Next morning, accompanied by the boy, who was receptionist and porter, I reached the bus at about 5.45am, to find it simply crowded. The boy bought me a ticket and found me a seat right at the back on a long seat. Opposite to this long seat were two small seats that faced the back of the bus; these seats were very close together and there was insufficient room for everyone's legs. On my right was a young wife of a soldier with a tiny baby. They both had terrible colds. Opposite to her sat a plump girl of about nineteen who was very sick; this made the soldier's wife sick. This nearly made me sick since they were not discreetly sick as the English were but they made a great deal of noise and were sick anywhere. I found a bottle of travel sick pills and quickly doled them out to these two. One of the men asked me if they were vitamins. Then a man a few seats away gave me his window seat so that I could have a view.

The countryside was attractive. To begin with we were in the mountains but as we wound down towards Titograd the grass became green and lush. There were bridges over a fast running stream and some of the peasants' cottages were picturesque. The weather began to get warm and on reaching Titograd at about 8.30am the sun was already hot.

SEVEN

Titograd

Titograd was grim. It had obviously been badly hit by the war and reconstruction was still in progress. The streets were hot and dusty and there were heaps of rubble. The buildings were uniform. There were many people about; they were shabbily dressed and the atmosphere was a great change from Dalmatia. It was rather depressing and sordid and the people gave one the impression of being hostile.

I asked some men the way to the Railway Station: they just walked on. I then asked some others if they spoke English, German or French and they disappeared likewise. I then asked a group of youths the same question. They just stared and were about to go when a comrade of theirs appeared and he spoke French. With many gesticulations he pointed out the route to the station.

The way led out of the town and into the country, and past a little farmstead. It was hot walking and I saw a lame young man with a stick and asked him how much further the station was.

He could not speak English but he understood and walked with me.

The station consisted of a very temporary low wooden building divided into two rooms. In one room was the ticket office. The other was a bar. The two girls in the ticket office only spoke Serbo-Croat, so only by pointing to words in my dictionary, which was a very lengthy business, was I able to buy a ticket from Titograd to Sarajevo. The train only had second and third class seats so I bought a second class ticket and managed to get the tourist fifty per cent reduction. By now there was quite a miscellaneous crowd around me. I then explained by signs that I wanted to eat and was taken in the other room.

In this room there was a bar with tables and chairs where army and air force officers and other ranks and some civilians were drinking. I sat at a table and was immediately surrounded by servicemen, who, although they could speak no English, ordered slivovic and in the twinkling of an eye there were six glasses lined up. I drank one glass and insisted that I must have coffee since it was now 9.30am and I had had nothing to eat or drink that morning. A small sticky cup of Turkish coffee was produced and then I asked for bread. The small, kind and dirty waiter gave me a huge slice of black bread so I then asked for jam or butter. They could only offer a tin of sardines. I therefore got out a box of Kraft cheese, the only edible thing I had besides one orange, and asked for a knife. This caused great consternation. There was only one knife, and that a sort of boy scout's knife. I assured them that that would do admirably and, cutting the Kraft into thick slices, I ate bread and cheese with an amused audience. They wanted to know if it was butter so I explained that it was cheese and gave some of them a taste.

I then managed to get a glass of water but before I had had two mouthfuls, it was removed and substituted by a glass of wine. I could not be ungracious, so I thanked them and drank the wine. The atmosphere was most friendly and jovial.

One army captain sitting at the next table spoke a little German, so we said a few words to each other. Sitting at my table was the lame civilian who had shown me the way to the station, an air force lieutenant who only spoke Serbo-Croat, and an air force corporal who spoke a very little English, fluent Russian and of course Serbo-Croat.

The corporal asked me if I was English, where I came from, where I was going, if I liked Yugoslavia, what did I think of the people, what was England like, had I a sister, what was she doing and where was she. He translated my answers to the other two at my table. It seemed that I was the first English woman they had met and as well as being curious they were very anxious for news from outside Yugoslavia. The lame civilian now said farewell and left us.

The air force officer and corporal had a friend, also an air force officer, who was a teacher of English. The officer went to find him but he had gone for the day to a neighbouring Air Force Station. Great use was made of my Serbo-Croat dictionary, for without it intelligent conversation could never have been held.

The air force lieutenant was a pilot, and so was their teacher of English. The corporal was training to be a pilot and hoped to take his examinations soon. He then said very softly, 'When I am pilot, my friend,' pointing to the lieutenant opposite, 'my teacher and I in one aeroplane to England.' He then opened my dictionary and pointed to the word 'safety'. I smiled and murmured 'yes'.

I said I must get onto the platform in case the train went, but I was pressed to drink up the row of slivovic which I explained I could not do because I was not used to alcoholic drinks at that hour. I was then given a very sweet liqueur as a great treat. I therefore had to drink it, regardless.

The train arrived on time at 10am. The air force pilot and corporal found me a seat in an empty, dusty and very dirty second class compartment. It was worse than any of our worst third class in England. They dusted the compartment as best they could and, having discovered that I did not arrive at Sarajevo until 9.30am next day, a matter of twenty-three and a half hours, I enquired whether there was a dining car, but was told that there was not. The corporal then ran into his barracks (the airfield was just beside the railway station) and came back with half a loaf of black bread. I was most grateful and now felt well set for the journey with this, a little Kraft cheese and an orange.

All the people who had been in the room drinking had now assembled outside the station (there were no platforms) and as the train moved out of the station they waved me goodbye. This was an exceptionally slow train, stopping at every station. The real compensation was the scenery which was simply magnificent. The route wound first westwards to Dubrovnik then northwards through Mostar and then eastwards to Sarajevo.

I wandered through the empty train exploring. All compartments were equally filthy but the lavatory was revolting. I am quite certain that it had never been cleaned, let alone swept, since the train was built, and it was an old train.

I was not alone long. An army lieutenant, small, dark and greasy with an untidy, creased and dirty uniform, joined me. He spoke a very little bad French. He volunteered the information, and took great pains to explain, that the reason why there was an armed policeman on the train was because there was a great deal of theft by violence, and that even at that moment someone in Titograd might be telephoning to a friend that an English woman was on the train and someone would get on at a later station and rob me at night. I did not like this man, and fervently hoped that I should not have to spend the night alone with him. We went through many long tunnels through the mountains and then the compartment was in complete darkness. I felt apprehensive.

After a little while we were joined by a fair, handsome air

force captain. He spoke a little German and was friendly. His home was in Mostar where he usually spent the weekend; he was on his way there now to see his wife. They had only been married a very short time and he had many photographs of her. She looked most attractive.

Soon we were joined by two young women and their mother. One of the young women was dark, small and fidgety. The other was very large and fair. She had a great deal of fair hair which waved naturally and she never seemed to weary of combing it. She wore a revealing sleeveless jumper and was really rather voluptuous. Their mother was large and heavily built with grey hair. They had brought two large string bags full of food and two large bottles of water.

The railway went through magnificent mountain scenery that stretched far away on the left and towered up on the right. There were no trees and very little grass: just stony mountain vastnesses.

During the journey all these people chattered, especially the two young women and the army officer. The older woman had constant violent coughing attacks and spat at intervals. The women's meal was extremely substantial. They had two large loaves of black bread, a great deal of meat and ham, eggs and cheese. I finished my Kraft cheese and ate some bread. I was rather dry, as the day was exceedingly hot, so I ate the orange. The fair young woman cut a tremendous cake into very large pieces and gave me a piece. It was good and light and I think it was a special Easter cake.

Soon after it was dark we had to change trains. We spent one and half hours in a crowded buffet where the two men bought we women coffee and behaved in a very western way. When the other train came in the air force officer leapt on and got me a seat. The train was crowded but the same people that were with me in the previous train all managed to get into my carriage and we continued our journey.

The air force captain bade me farewell at Mostar. It was now about midnight and I dozed fitfully until early morning. I then cleaned my face as best I could and waited until we arrived at Sarajevo at about 9am on Sunday.

EIGHT

Sarajevo

Sarajevo was a slightly bewildering town for anyone arriving at the railway station for the first time. It was quite a distance from the centre of the town and, although I walked a fair way down a number of streets, I could not see which road led to the town. Finally I asked a policeman how I reached the Hotel Europa and he showed me which tram to catch.

Although I repeated 'Hotel Europa' many times with varying accents, no one in the tram looked as if they had ever heard of it (and I knew it to be the largest and best hotel in Sarajevo). So I sat firmly down, gave the conductor some dinars, shrugged my shoulders and he gave me a ticket and change with a shrug of his shoulders and a smile.

After we had rattled a good way down a wide road with trees and large buildings on either side, the tram stopped because there was a procession proceeding slowing down the road. The conductor told me I had better get off and walk and he gave my case to a scruffy young man and told him to take me to the hotel.

This man set off at a great walking speed and I discovered that he was intent on taking me to the Hotel Posta. I firmly told him I was going to the Hotel Europa and, after a little hesitation, we set off again in the same direction as the procession.

It was Sunday morning and the streets were full of people just taking the air. We overtook the procession which was marching slowly and dejectedly behind a military band playing a slow march. The people in the streets paid no attention to the procession and were mostly shop gazing. After what seemed to me a very long walk we arrived at the Hotel Europa.

The Hotel was large, dark, comfortable and clean. The receptionist and some of the waiters spoke English. Being tired and dirty I asked for a bath and a bed to get a few hours sleep in now, for I knew I should be travelling again all night. When I went to have a bath, I walked into the bathroom to find the door unlocked and a large, fat man sitting in his shirt doing up his suspenders. I apologised and withdrew. He did not seem in the least surprised and quietly went on dressing. I think he was German. Having finally bathed I slept for a few hours, then had luncheon and went for a walk.

I visited Putnik and bought a ticket for the journey from Sarajevo to Trieste. Taking advantage of a tourist visa, which gave one the concession of fifty per cent reduction on the railways, I decided to travel first class. The poor young Putnik clerk could not find any first class tickets until he had nearly ransacked the office and after one hour I emerged with the ticket.

I then wandered around the town. It was too hot to walk far but I thought Sarajevo was quite a reasonable town and large and well administered for Yugoslavia. There were some picturesque buildings, some gardens, squares and good wide streets. The buildings were large and well built. The town looked substantial and prosperous.

I enquired from the receptionist in the hotel as to the reason for the procession I had seen earlier in the day. Had someone well known died? The receptionist explained that it was a celebration. He laughed when I told him I thought that someone had died because everyone was looking so miserable, especially those in the procession.

I had a hasty tea, paid my bill and asked for a taxi. A large American car arrived, supplied by Putnik, and with it came the boy who had taken so long finding the first class ticket. He said he had just come to wish me a good journey and he saw me off with many bows and waves.

The taxi driver was friendly. When we reached the station he scattered the porters and carried my bag himself, found me an empty compartment and raved over the beauties of Sarajevo, especially in winter when no one worked but went off to the mountains to ski; they even had a ski-lift. He asked me to return some day and assured me that I only had to let him know I was back and he could drive me whenever I wished. He then returned to his taxi.

Feeling tired, I decided to spend the journey sleeping. The

train was due to leave at about 5pm and get to Slavonski Brod at 1.30am the following day. But before the train left Sarajevo a tall, elderly, kindly looking man came into my compartment and, on discovering that I was English and could not speak Serbo-Croat (he could neither speak French nor German), he found a friend in the second class compartment who could speak German and a little French and brought him along to my compartment. We shook hands and exchanged a few words then he changed his second-class ticket into a first-class one and joined the kind, elderly man and myself in our compartment.

NINE

Return to Trieste

The train pulled slowly out of the station as we left Sarajevo and headed north. The latest arrival had a very merry round face, brown laughing eyes, was about six feet tall, was robust and wore a beret and a brown tweed suit and tweed overcoat. He explained that he was forty years old, had never been married and was a lawyer. He then immediately asked me if I was married and when he learnt that I was not, he straightway proposed. He said that I need only live in Sarajevo for a few months of every year and then I could go to England. He would very much like to come to England also. He had plenty of money and I could even work if I wanted to!

'I have not seen such a thing before; I shall not see such a thing again. You must marry me,' he declared.

I was very amused, but realised that he was in earnest so replied, 'But this is so sudden.' He said that he knew he wanted to marry me and surely I knew also. He seemed to have no conception of the very different lives we led. All this time the elderly man sat smiling in a corner. Having thought that I could not have understood him (our conversation was in stilted German and French) he fetched a friend from the second class compartment. She was the wife of a doctor and was Viennese and spoke excellent English.

She told me that this man wanted to marry me and confirmed that he was unmarried. She then said that she was getting off at a little station before Slavonski Brod and that I could stay with her for the night and we could get married in the morning, and that if I needed her any more she would be only too willing to help. She returned to her husband and children. She was well educated, attractive and charming. Although she was married to a Yugoslav, she spent most of her time in Austria.

I finally managed to make this man realise that I did not want to get married. He found it difficult to believe and asked me to think it over and to write to him. At about 10pm this man, the elderly man, the Viennese woman and her family all left the train. I then settled down to sleep.

At Slavonski Brod I had to wait forty minutes for the Simplon Express. The night was dark and rather cold so I decided that I had better spend the time in the waiting room. The station was dreary and dirty and the only place lit up was the buffet, so in I went. It was hot, airless and crowded with people and there was a dense haze of tobacco smoke hanging just above their heads. There were two women in the buffet, the rest were men who were sitting at tables drinking and smoking. The people were shabbily dressed and what I noticed most was the drabness of the scene; they were just a dull mass; no one caught the eye or stood out from the rest even by the way they dressed. The officers were very much smarter than those I saw on the Dalmatian coast and their uniforms were in much better condition.

Amidst mild curiosity I searched for a chair, and finally found one and ordered coffee. Immediately a little, thin, middle aged man asked me if I was English, where I had come from and whither I was going. When I told him I was waiting for the Simplon Express he produced a timetable and checked on the time of its arrival. He was a station master and was going to Zagreb. He was a mild little man and we chatted of this and that.

Suddenly a porter approached and announced the arrival of the train at the same time as it drew into the station. People leapt up and rushed to the door. What a moment before had been a still, colourless mass had suddenly become chaos. By the time I had put on my coat and collected my luggage, the buffet was empty. There were no platforms, one just climbed up into the train. There were bunches of people still pushing their way into train doors and a soldier with an Alsatian dog on a leash walked beside the train to a group of people pushing their way in, and stood there watching.

There were other soldiers with Alsatian dogs walking under the train to ensure that no one was escaping from the country by sitting on the axles of the coaches.

I found an empty first class compartment and, being very tired as it was 2am, I turned out the light, shut the door and stretched full length on a seat and decided to sleep. After the usual interruptions of the ticket collector and the policeman inspecting passports, I was just sinking into unconsciousness when I became aware of someone in the compartment. I opened my eyes to see a tall, young man standing in the dark compartment, looking at me. I did not like the way he looked. I sprang up and asked him in French what he wanted. He replied in a language I did not understand and did not move. It was quite obvious that he was not the sort of person to travel first class, so I pushed him gently towards and out of the door. He only protested mildly but I firmly closed the door and he went away.

Considering the situation, I thought it unwise to remain alone in the compartment, especially since I was so tired. I therefore went into the next compartment where there were already four passengers fast asleep. I sat down and dozed uncomfortably until morning.

At Zagreb, Mr Marchant, the British Consul General, joined the train. He was off to Switzerland to do some Spring skiing.

I shared a table with a German for breakfast. He was a greedy and noisy eater so I made certain that I did not share his table for luncheon. At the Yugoslav frontier the officials could not understand how I was not given a money declaration form when I entered Yugoslavia. However, they were very friendly and finally with a shrug of their shoulders, they went on their way. After a good lunch (by Army standards) I reached Trieste at 1.30pm.

The sun was still shining and had done so for the whole of this trip.

THE LOST ANATOLIAN
KINGDOM 1954

THE LOST ANATOLIAN
KINGDOM 1954

ONE

The Lost Anatolian Kingdom

It was just a usual Saturday morning. I had breakfasted late and was now sipping coffee while gazing from the window of the Excelsior Hotel in Trieste at the Adriatic Sea. The sun was shining and all was serenity.

I picked up *The Times* newspaper. It was the thin air-mail edition dated 8th May 1954. Glancing at the leaders on page seven, I noted that butter rationing in England was due to end this weekend, but it was the headline 'Search for Lost Anatolian Kingdom' that caught my attention.

The Hittites had always fascinated me. They cropped up from time to time in articles, poetry, history and the Bible. Conquering, sacking, fierce and elusive, living romantically in the desert. They had been a great power in the north east of the Anatolian plateau with their capital at Bogazkoy. I instantly decided to travel in the area and finish at Bogazkoy.

The article showed that more excavations were about to take place so I decided to take time from work and discover if I could join in a little excavation, if they would have me. I felt elated. I decided to go to Istanbul, and then Ankara. In order to absorb the flavour of Anatolia I planned to travel to Konya, Adana, Tarsus, Maras, Malatya, Sivas and Kayseri and finally reach Bogazkoy.

In 1954 England was very English. I had only been to Lapland, Yugoslavia, the Balkans and Singapore, Thailand and Malaysia. It was no great problem for a woman to travel alone in these countries. I was quite unprepared for the way of life of the people in Central Turkey. No one had warned me so I wore what I would now consider the most unsuitable clothing, but what was normal for European women at that time. No one had given me any idea what Asia Minor was like.

I packed the minimum. Some cotton dresses worn below the knee, sleeveless or short sleeves, and round scooped necklines. No stockings. Just sandals, a woollen cardigan, two long, cool nightdresses and a duffle coat.

At the time I was working in Trieste, with a British/American intelligence set-up. It was not until 12th September that I could get away. The British Military Attaché, Tom Sedgwick, offered me a lift to Belgrade. I accepted gladly, and Tom and I left Trieste at 9am.

The car was a new Humber Hawk with CD plates which allowed us to pass the Italian and Yugoslav frontiers without delay. We took the main road to Ljubljana where we collected Dushan, Tom's chauffeur. Dushan was looking very smart, having just bought the conventional chauffeur's cap, which we duly admired. He was young, dark, pale and stolid, and was inclined to drive at a steady seventy-five miles an hour regardless of pigs, hens, children, cows, etc. Tom studied a paper on Guatemala and the United Nations during the entire journey.

We had a puncture just outside Ljubljana, where three strange vehicles passed us. They were little cars, just like cockroaches with two tiny wheels in front and one behind, with handlebars instead of a steering wheel, and a roof like an aeroplane cockpit. There was room for the driver only and luggage behind. They could do sixty miles an hour and were German. A one-armed man on a motorcycle seemed to be in charge of them.

We arrived in Belgrade at 9.30pm, where Tom's sister told us that Carmen Forbes had expected me earlier, and so had arranged for me to go to a dinner engagement with her. However, it being so late, I dined with Tom and then went round to the Forbes and later returned about midnight.

Next day was the normal Belgrade social round: coffee with Madame Helb, the Dutch Minister's wife; tea with the Dutch Military Attaché's wife, a British girl; drinks and dinner with the Lerwalls, our Air Attaché, where I met Air Vice Marshal Brooks on his way to Baghdad. The following day was socially quieter: tea with the French Minister's wife (a great strain on my French); cocktails at the Menes, US Military Attaché giving a farewell party for the Israeli Minister; and Carmen had arranged a small dinner party where I met my old friend, Phillipe of the French News Agency.

During dinner I decided to leave Belgrade next morning at 7.30am. When I announced this Peter Forbes protested that one couldn't just slip away into Asia Minor, one must plan. But I knew that unless I wrenched myself away, I should just remain day after day. Phillipe got his chauffeur, who kept the petty cash, to buy me a return ticket to Istanbul, and next day, at 7.15am, I arrived on the crowded Belgrade station.

The Simplon Orient Express was crowded and hot. Even every seat in the second class coaches seemed full. But the moment Peter left me to fetch my suitcase, three little men ran at me and assured me that there was room in their carriage! I decided on a fat, happy, middle-aged, English-speaking Turk who stowed away my belongings in a crowded compartment. There were nine in the carriage, all men except for myself. Very few women seemed to travel east of Belgrade. There were four Yugoslavs: two workers, a factory manager at Skoplje and an army captain, a small mousy German who spoke a little English and was on his way to Athens. He described himself as a 'representative'. Finally, there were two Turks who bulged and took up a seat and a half each in the already crowded carriage. The one who spoke English had been on business to the Zagreb Fair and the other was an elderly, well-dressed man who was a Turkish refugee and had settled in Salonika (Greece) since 1924.

The Turk who spoke English fed me throughout the journey on orange squash. During the journey to Salonika, which took seventeen hours, there was continual chatter in the carriage.

The countryside was dull. Flattish land with dried up looking crops of sweet corn and sunflowers. Everywhere looked brown and dry in the boiling sun and there were no hills or mountains during the first part of the journey.

By mid-day the crowded carriage was unbearably hot, and the only relief was to stand in the sunny corridor where there was a draught. I lunched in the restaurant car. It was a rather colourless luncheon, and the dining car even hotter than the carriage.

We reached Nis at 5pm, and Skoplje about 9pm. Between these two places the countryside became more interesting with the Bulgarian mountains on the left and the Albanian ones to the right. The landscape was one vast and barren chain of mountains on either side, but at some distance from the train.

The landscape now became wilder and more barren and the railway ran close to the hills. The full moon shining from behind the Bulgarian mountains made the countryside look dark, lonely and mysterious. I was sorry to arrive at Salonika and leave the moonlit mountains, but at the same time I was glad not to be out alone in that mysterious blackness.

TWO

Salonika

Just before we entered the railway station the Turk explained that the Turkish refugee owned a hotel in Salonika and that he had offered him a bed since all hotels were full because of the Trade Fair, and that the only alternative would be to sleep in the railway station. The Turk had turned down the offer because he said I must have his bed since it was more suitable for him to sleep at the station. He then added, 'He very good man, he very fat man, all fat man good man, you go with him, he look after you.'

I thanked him and explained that I hoped a friend would meet me and would have arranged something. Whereat they replied that they would stand by in case my friend did not arrive, because it was not suitable for me to be left stranded. Actually, I was met by Richard Muirhead, a young well-washed Gunner officer whom I had met briefly once before. I then thanked and bade farewell to the Turks and went off with Richard.

Richard was a delightful young man, with a charming wife

called Norma, and a six months old son, Nicholas. It being midnight, Norma and Nicholas were in bed and I soon went to bed myself.

At 9am next day I was awakened from a deep sleep by Norma bringing breakfast. Paddy Turnbull had telephoned and had put his car at my disposal, plus a corporal. Paddy had invited me to luncheon, and George Zacharias had invited me to dinner.

The day was hot and after a hasty cold bath and breakfast I went out with Corporal Brodie. He was a regular soldier who had signed on for twenty-two years, had so far done eighteen months, and was still thrilled by being in the army. He considered being stationed at Salonika as one long holiday and enjoyed it immensely.

He took me to the International Industrial Fair. We visited the British, Russian and Greek Pavilions. What impressed me most was the gigantic Russian lorry that could carry twenty-five tons. I had never seen anything quite so massive and it would take about six men to lift one wheel. We then went into the town and visited the bookshop; this I gathered was Corporal Brodie's pet spot. It was now time for coffee.

I asked to be taken to the top of the hill to a ruined castle. The corporal had never been there, but eventually we made the driver understand. We first visited a monastery where there were masses of icons and peacocks. The peacocks have no tails in September, but they grow again in the spring. We went on to the ruin; all that remained was the thick Roman wall. Inside was a Turkish village with the people living in hovels. I took a photograph of the town from the top of the wall. It was now time to go to the Turnbulls for luncheon.

Elsa Turnbull was most attractive. Besides Paddy and herself there was only George Zacharias there. It was most enjoyable. Their house was on the sea shore and was well furnished. We had an unforgettably excellent wine and a Greek dish of rice with nuts.

After luncheon I went with Paddy to the office, and was introduced to two baby donkeys, geese, hens, an Alsatian dog, two cats and the other British officer, Ronnie Curtis, who was to join us in Trieste in December. He was very keen, serious, without much sense of humour, and with an inferiority complex about being in the Royal Army Service Corps. He had previously been in the Indian Army.

We left the office and were taken by Richard and Norma to watch a tennis match between Salonika and Austria. There we met Paddy. Ronnie took me to Cooks where we discovered that the next through train to Istanbul was in three days time. There was, however, a way of getting there by train that meant changing at Alexandropolis and Pythion. I decided that time was getting short; therefore I would leave next morning.

There were fourteen at George's dinner party which was given in an outdoor restaurant. It was fun. We dined, wined and danced and I tried some Ouzo , the Greek national drink. I didn't like it.

Next morning, amid protests from Richard, I left at 6.30am, and caught the local train at 7am for Alexandropolis.

THREE

Alexandropolis to Pythion

We did not reach Alexandropolis until 6pm. The journey was excessively hot, especially since there was a girl in the carriage who was ill, and her mother insisted on the window being closed.

At Alexandropolis all the railway officials told me that I must stay the night and go on next morning. But I insisted that I must go on that night. They said that there was no train, until a Greek passenger asked me in French if he could help. I explained that I had to go on to Istanbul that night. He said to come with him and immediately had my baggage loaded onto a carriage and pair and off we galloped across Alexandropolis, at break-neck speed, wiping natives off the horses hooves. I had no idea where we were going, but eventually we arrived at the sea, and running right beside the sea was a single track railway. It was the most exciting, and frightening, drive of my life.

The Greek gave my luggage to a porter and sat me on a chair near a coffee bar and told me the train would be in in ten minutes. Then with an *au revoir* and a wave, my gallant horseman galloped away. I was immediately surrounded by little Greek soldiers, but the owner of the coffee bar, a tall, lean, stern old man, swept them away and stood beside me until the train arrived.

The crush through the barrier was frightening. There were no railway officials and everyone pushed, shouted, dug and plunged. There were police standing beside the train trying to stop people from being pushed between the train and the platform. Fortunately my porter had a seat for me and when the train, of only two coaches, was crammed full, it left the station and waited outside. We continued in this cramped state for four hours until reaching the Greek/Turkish frontier at Python about 11pm.

We should then have caught another train immediately for Istanbul but there had been an accident that day on the line just outside Istanbul and the train would be three hours late.

The Greek customs officials and frontier police were charming. They found a chair for me and placed it among the peasants, babies, dogs, melons and bundles. Then they produced an English-speaking customs official who took me off to a restaurant for refreshment. He asked me if I was 'Miss' or 'a lady'. When I told him 'Miss', he asked if I was going to Istanbul as 'Miss' to come back as 'lady'. I assured him that that was not the aim of my journey, but I don't think he was convinced.

Eventually, at 2am, the train arrived and we were all bundled into a third class coach which had hard wooden seats. The Turkish officials immediately descended. They were quick and courteous and just asked me to sign a blank form; they filled in the rest afterwards. I had the impression that they did not take their duties too seriously.

I told every official that I had a second class ticket and showed it to them, but they all returned with the same answer, very apologetically, that there was no seat. Then a fellow passenger, an energetic young Turk with a good flow of French, told me he would find me a place. He returned saying that I could have a couchette for three Turkish lire extra, about four shillings and six pence. I was very grateful to him.

In the couchette were two Greeks with a dog and two Germans with a small boy (all female, except for the boy, and I don't know about the dog).

I awakened at 7am, having slept soundly, and discovered that everyone else was up and dressed. I went to sleep again for another hour, and was dressed and ready about 9am. On the right now was the beginning of the Marmara Sea. It was quite the bluest blue I had ever seen, and it seemed to remain so all the summer. It certainly was beautiful, and the Turks had a lido where the fashionable people from Istanbul came.

FOUR

Istanbul

The train followed the sea round and finally stopped in Istanbul station at 11.30am.

There to meet me was a British sergeant, with a British Embassy employee who had a Turkish mother. He certainly must have taken after her in looks. He was very useful because he had a huge official car. These two had been waiting for me since 7.35am. Major Bigwood was away so the sergeant took it upon himself to do all that he thought should be done. And he was excellent.

We swept through the busy, hot Istanbul streets to the British Embassy where I discovered that the Consul General, Leslie Potts, whom Bill Tailyour said I was to see, was away. My other contact, Major Bigwood, was also away and Terry Malloy was in Ankara. I then visited the press office and asked if Mike Richards was in town. Fortunately he was living in Istanbul, and was coming into the Embassy that morning, so the sergeant, Mr Callus (the one with the car) and I went off to find a cheap hotel for me.

We eventually found a room in a tiny hotel called the Murat, used by British and Americans. Mr Callus drove off and the sergeant and I walked back to the Embassy to meet Mike. We walked because the sergeant insisted that by walking I would learn the way much better and it was important not to get lost. As we walked he told me that since I had no friends in Istanbul I should leave as soon as possible for it was not safe for me to be alone and I must not go out after dark.

When I arrived at the British Embassy to meet Mike I also met a young journalist called Bill Smyley. A quiet, dark, pleasant young man who said he was driving to Ankara and would take me. Mike said immediately that since his house was on the way to Ankara Bill Smyley, Mr Wyatt (the assistant press attaché) and I should come for lunch with him tomorrow and Bill and I should stay the night and leave early for Ankara next morning. I accepted this offer gratefully.

The sergeant walked back with me to the Murat Hotel and I took myself off to lunch at the Park Hotel. It was modern, clean and good. It was the best one in Ankara. I had an excellent lunch which was the set lunch and it cost me fifteen shillings.

The weather was excessively hot so I rested after lunch and remained in the hotel all the evening except for going to the embassy twice to ring Major Malloy (Assistant Military Attaché at Ankara) to ask him to book me a room at an inexpensive hotel in Ankara.

Istanbul suffered from acute water shortage. There was never any hot water and in the Murat there was no cold either. There was only one main street which was dingy, dirty and overcrowded. There were many smaller streets. The great charm about the city was to see it from the Bosphorus, the Marmara Sea and the Golden Horn. Its skyline of domes and minarets was enchanting and there are many other impressive buildings. The weather was perfect with a cloudless blue sky which made the sea intensely blue.

The next day at 10am Mr Wyatt and I climbed into Bill Smyley's small Standard Eight motor car. The back was piled with luggage because he was driving to Colombo to embark on a boat for Hong Kong where he was to be the assistant editor of the Hong Kong and Morning Post. He was hoping to meet his parents in Colombo who were missionaries on their way to an island in the China Sea. We boarded the ferry to cross the Bosphorus and reach the other part of Istanbul, and so we left Europe behind and I landed in Asia approximately where Florence Nightingale landed: at Scutari. The filth, squalor and poverty are still extreme and one realised anew how brave she must have been.

The main road was appalling. It was narrow, full of pot-holes and the tram lines ran on either side leaving only the smallest gap for cars in the middle. We bumped along this road past a very large Arab cemetery on the left, full of ancient cypress trees. On the outskirts of Istanbul, not far from the Marmara Sea, we found Mike's bungalow. Mike and Benino were awaiting us with a vodka fizz and an excellent luncheon cooked by Mike. He and Benino had only just moved into the house. They had no servant, so we washed up, rested and prepared the evening meal. Then Bill put his camp bed up in the study, I had the maid's room and we went to bed early because we were getting up at next day at 5am.

The next day, soon after 6am, Bill and I left for Ankara and drove off into the dawn, and unknown Anatolia. The road was not well sign-posted to Ankara and, after many inquiries, and a few wrong turns, we finally found the correct road.

Just outside Istanbul one realised that this was indeed Asia Minor. Poverty, filth, donkeys, women with their faces covered and working in the fields or carrying heavy loads, and masses of men, some working but many doing nothing. The road ran along the beautiful Marmara coast for a time and then left the sea, and crossed the plain to climb a steep mountain pass onto a plateau. We stopped when we saw a colourful group living in tents. They had many tiny, dirty, hungry and sore-covered children. They showed us a cock-fight and gave me a tiny wet bundle of a baby to hold. We gave the children barley sugar and a little money.

We stopped for lunch at a mountain village called Bolu, and here I had my first real Turkish meal: squares of meat on a skewer, stuffed eggplant and green vegetables stuffed, also tomatoes and peppers. Afterwards the most delicious cream cheese that I have ever tasted. During lunch we had the car serviced because we had travelled along an incredibly dusty road.

Bolu was a market town and very picturesque. The streets were crowded with people and donkeys, but few people seemed to be doing anything; they just stood around talking.

We drove on through the mountains. The scenery was lovely. The day was hot and clear and we could see for miles. It gets dark quite early, about 6pm, and once the sun has set, it is exceedingly cold in the mountains.

High up on a plateau on a terrible dust road, the car broke down at about 7pm. There was a strong wind sweeping across from the north. On looking inside the bonnet, Bill discovered that the continual shaking and jolting had unloosed all bolts and nuts, etc, some of which had fallen off altogether. By now a lorry had appeared and the driver and his mate came to help. With the use of some hairpins, bits of rag and other odds and ends, they had the car going again and off we went.

We stopped at various wayside cafés for tea or coffee. These cafés were shacks with a few wooden chairs and tables, and they were delighted to see strangers. They make excellent sweet Turkish coffee or tea without milk but with plenty of sugar and served in glasses. We saw the lights of Ankara about 9pm.

In Ankara, I telephoned the British Embassy and discovered that they had booked me a room in the Celnick Palace Hotel, a cheap but central and clean place.

FIVE

Ankara

After the fifteen hour drive, we reached Ankara. It seemed a very large place with its mass of street lights stretching far. It had a fine boulevard and gardens and an imposing statue of Attaturk on horseback with four soldiers standing around it in varying dramatic attitudes. At one end of this main boulevard were the shops and my hotel and towards the other end were all the foreign Embassies. It was a three mile walk from my hotel to the British Embassy along this Boulevard.

On arriving at the hotel I discovered that I was sharing a room with a young woman who was able to speak English. Bill managed to get a bed in the corridor. We both went upstairs to wash.

My stable companion was a small, very dark, skinny Arab woman. She was strange and probably a lesbian. She asked me if she could help me undress and then commented on my English figure and bemoaned her own thinness saying that Turkish men liked women with flesh. I advised her to find an

American because their women spend much money trying to become slim. She could not do enough for me and was constantly wanting to touch me.

While I was washing and changing, the hotel manager, George, who spoke frightful American English, and blasphemed constantly, came into the room without knocking. The Arab girl, in her nightdress, accepted this quite normally. I hastily completed my toilet and went downstairs; George followed me and asked me to have dinner with him. I said I was sorry, I could not do so, and went off in search of Bill. I found Bill in the corridor beside his bed in his pants. I explained my predicament and he said he would be down in five minutes.

We ate in a tiny restaurant where we first went into the kitchen and pointed to what we wanted. We then went to a pastry shop and sampled everything there. All pastries were swamped in honey and there was only one I liked; it was ground walnuts in layers of pastry soaked in honey. We went to another shop and drank Turkish coffee, then drove to the park and walked. The flowers were mostly tobacco flowers and smelled very sweet in the night air. It was cold and pleasant walking and, having walked round the lake and over the bridges, we returned.

In the hotel I decided to wash my hair in the wash hand basin and have a bath. Having washed my hair, I discovered that the bathroom was locked so I rang for the key. When the key was brought I locked myself in but to my dismay there was only scalding hot water. I opening the windows to let the steam out and there was a knock on the door and the manager's voice asking,

'Are you having a nice bath?'

I replied angrily, 'No!' and explained that there was no cold water.

'Unlock the door and let me in,' said the voice outside.

'Not at the moment,' I replied and put on some clothes. I then unlocked the door and swept angrily out of the bathroom, explaining to George that I would have one in the morning.

'You do not want a bath, you want whiskey,' said George. I declined, and locked myself in the bedroom. The Arab girl was asleep, so I quietly opened the window and got into bed.

Next morning, while I was standing in my undies, in walked George again without knocking. 'Go away' I said. 'I am not dressed.' And he went.

The Arab girl said soothingly, 'Do not mind him, Mademoiselle. He very good man. He not touch, he only look. He like look very much.' I explained that I had not come to Turkey to have strange men in my bedroom. At that moment Terry Malloy rang and invited me to luncheon. Bill rang and said he was downstairs having breakfast. Was I coming? He would take me to the embassy.

When I told Bill about George's overtures he told me not to hesitate to find him and to ring him if I was ever in any difficulties, and he would come. I was most grateful because it was blatantly obvious that I could not be alone in Ankara, for even when I was with Bill it was bad enough because the Turkish men looked at me in a way that made me feel uncomfortable.

Mike had given me an introduction to Mr Butler, the press attaché. He advised me to visit the south coast and not to go elsewhere. I then walked three miles through the blazing sun back to the hotel and arrived hot and exhausted, but just in time for Terry.

Terry and his father were both delightful, and they took me to luncheon at the one large restaurant in Ankara. It was rather like a dilapidated English club, with everyone eating in a vast dismal hall, but the food and service were good.

After lunch we went up the hill to see the memorial to Attaturk. It was a huge, rectangular pillared building. All the pillars were square and had no capitals or bases. Beyond the pillars there were wrought bronze gates on three sides. Through the gates there was a vast hall with a mosaic ceiling and walls of white unpolished marble. At the far end, there was a large bay window, and it was here that the great, black tomb of Attaturk was erected. Before the tomb was a golden wreath which had now become a shrine for many Turks. Along the winding drive up to the tomb trees had been planted given by many countries in memory of Attaturk. The British government had given English yew trees.

We went back to Terry's office where we discussed my projected tour, and discovered that there were only two Simplon Orient Expresses from Istanbul back to Trieste during the week.

Terry sent off a wire to Trieste asking permission for me to return a day later so that I could fit in my tour. He advised me not to go to Bogaskoy. He said it was too difficult without one's own car. But he raised no objection to my going to Konya, Adana, Tarsus, Maras, Malatya, Sivas, Kayseri, and back to Ankara. All this was difficult but possible. We returned to his house and had tea with his children, Timmy and Kitty. He drove me back to my hotel at 6pm, and wished me good luck.

George met me inside the hotel and asked me to dine with him. I said I was dining with my friend (Bill) and went to my room. Next moment George entered.

'I like you very much,' he said, leeringly.

'Go away!' I said, backing towards the door. He followed, getting very near. I moved backwards towards the door. Leaning against it with my hands behind me, I took the key out, while still facing George.

He was fat, red, hairless, with small pale blue eyes and covered in sweat. He was breathing on me. With all my force I pushed him away, slipped out of the door, quickly pulled it shut and locked it on the outside.

George banged and shouted. Some people passing down the corridor asked me what all the noise was about.

'I think someone must be locked in somewhere,' I replied casually, while continuing downstairs to the reception. I handed in the key of my room to reception as usual. Bill was waiting for me, and we left the hotel.

After Bill and I had had supper, we wandered around the town. It was really quite small, and all the shops were tiny, and mostly sold things to eat. We bought some nut nougat and what seemed like bars of birdseed with honey. It was very good.

I told Bill of my proposed trip, and he said that as it began roughly in the direction he was going, he didn't mind going a little out of his way, and he would give me a lift as far as possible. This I gladly accepted and we left next morning at 5.30am, heading for Konya, to penetrate the Anatolian Kingdom.

SIX

Konya

We drove into a beautiful dawn along an excellent road and it
was only where the Turks were widening and improving the road
that we had any difficulty. Just now, every road seemed to be in
the process of being widened and straightened owing to
American pressure for defence purposes. The most gigantic road
machinery, made in America or Germany was being used. They
put the under surface on these new wide roads, then ran out of
money and so left them, and the roads became corrugated. It
was hell driving on these roads in a small light car.

The road from Ankara to Konya was good and we drove into
a beautiful dawn that grew into a boiling hot day. There were
no trees to speak of in all this vast central part of Turkey. It was
just ranges of mountains and high plateaux with sometimes
roads that ran straight and could be seen for at least seven miles.
The land was of various colours but mostly a sandy red, and the
whole effect was of miles and miles of desert. Scattered
throughout were solitary water wells, just a beam and bucket

affair. There were no flowers and no butterflies. But plenty of buzzards and vultures.

On the plateaux there was a very thin layer of fertile soil as a top layer held there by a scanty growth of grass. Most ploughing was still done by oxen and a wooden prong, but tractors were also in use and these vast plateaux were being ploughed so the grass, the only thing that held the fertile soil down, was removed. Then the sweeping winds and many whirlwinds during the long, dry summer blew this layer away and, gradually, as the land was used for agriculture, it became desert. Its only real use would be for grazing sheep, goats, buffalo and geese. Everywhere the land had not been ploughed, there were a large number of herds grazing attended by shepherds, both boys and men with huge dogs. The shepherds were clad in the most ragged garments, but all looked extremely fit and cheerful. They were dark-skinned, with black eyes and hair. Some were playing on reed pipes and some had very strong catapults.

Hot and hungry, we arrived at Konya for luncheon and drove around looking for a restaurant. I saw a large white building just like a modern hotel with a garden of trees with large sunshades over tables and people sitting under them. Thinking this unbelievably wonderful, we parked the car and ran up many steps which led to the garden. Here we stopped, for all the people drinking were Turkish army officers. I asked if it was a restaurant. They were all smiles and a captain, who spoke French, assured me that it was. Another officer, a military police lieutenant, as his red arm band indicated, led us inside. We found ourselves in an officers' mess. There was great excitement among the orderlies and cooks, frightened-looking little dark men in khaki trousers and dirty white jackets.

Luncheon was soon ready and the orderlies produced squares of roasted meat, peppers, egg plant and rice. The great hunks of bread given by the orderlies were quickly spirited away by the officer and replaced by sliced bread. We were given iced beer to drink. There was also cheese and grapes.

The lieutenant and the French-speaking captain sat with us throughout the meal. They inquired into Bill's and my relationship. In halting French, Bill explained that we had only just met at the British Embassy, and that we were together only because we were travelling the same route. They found it unbelievable that comparative strangers of opposite sexes could do such a thing.

The French-speaking officer explained that he was a captain of artillery, and then asked us what we did. Bill explained that he was a journalist, and that I was an army captain. He was staggered at my profession, and more so when he discovered that I had been a captain a year longer than he had.

The lieutenant asked me if I would care to wash, and led me off to their hole in the floor. When I pointed out to him that the door had no fastening, a common failing of lavatory doors in Anatolia, the lieutenant stood on guard with his back to the door. When I emerged I washed my hands and was given a towel by an orderly who was standing there to attention holding the towel before him. I powdered my face and the lieutenant held my looking glass while I did so. It was all so very charming in such dark, smelly and sordid surroundings.

We joined the others and went outside and sat under umbrellas and drank sweet Turkish coffee while the orderlies took photographs of us with our cameras.

The captain of artillery explained that he was not married but that he was in love with someone else's wife, and showed us her photograph, from which he had cut the husband. The lieutenant's heart seemed unattached. After a little more conversation and a profusion of thanks, we left our hosts and went out into the blazing afternoon sun, in search of ancient ruins.

We were pounced upon by an earnest man with the appearance of a typical communist. He showed us some 12th century ruined walls and mosques. It was then that I discovered that many mosques were schools. They all had lovely ceilings worked in a coloured mosaic, a large square bath in the middle of the main room, smaller rooms off the main room and always one tomb, that of some famous ancient king, knight or priest. It was extremely hot, and, after having seen three identical mosques, I decided that it was time to be moving on again. By now we had two students on bicycles as escorts.

SEVEN

Adana & Eregli

Bill decided to get to Adana via Eregli, and one of the students accompanied us through Konya and put us on the right road. This road was narrow and really just an earth track full of potholes to begin with until we reached a part where it was being widened. Here huge machinery was at work and the whole vast new road was just ploughed-up dust. We were covered in dust, and seldom could go at more than ten miles an hour. At one place we had to take a diversion for about five miles.

The diversion consisted of taking a track across the desert plateau but since there were numerous tracks, it was difficult to decide on the best one. On two occasions we ended up in ditches and only extricated ourselves with difficulty. We were then advised by some peasants and, after skirting herds of goats and buffalo, found the road, but were unable to get on to it because of a high dust embankment. Finally, we came across a cut through the embankment and, with the aid of peasants who practically lifted the car, we reached the road.

Just here the road surface was hard but it was very corrugated so we could still go only slowly. The countryside was rather dull, just a desert plateau with isolated water pumps, and every now and again tiny villages with the hay stacked on the roofs, obviously to keep it out of reach of the cattle.

No journey has ever seemed so long and although it was already dark we were still far from Eregli. The headlights of the car picked up much nocturnal animal activity. Tiny four legged creatures scampered across the road or sat up and looked at us, and long things with short legs slunk into the grass beside the road. On either side of the road there were huge dogs with clipped ears out hunting, probably the only way for them to get food. They were great, powerful beasts who chased along beside the car at twenty-five mile an hour and seemed very fierce.

We had now reached a part of the road that had been churned up for repair, and the dust was so thick that the undercarriage of the car scraped through it. After a while, we came upon a stationary lorry in which there was a man and a most engaging boy. Both were very dark and dirty and the boy had a shock of black, tangled curls and a handsome, impish face. They told us to follow the diversion since the through road was impassable. We did so and drove through dust up to the radiator. After a short while the engine simply stopped. The night was dark and still, and one felt small and alone on a bleak, cold plateau with not a light in sight.

This was the first car Bill had possessed, and he had bought it new for the journey and had no idea why the engine had stopped, and certainly could not make it go again. He said we should have to remain where we were for the night and perhaps by morning, help might arrive.

It was 9.30pm, and very dark and cold. Bill suggested that I should have his camp bed and sleep beside the car, and he would just curl up inside. I protested that I could never sleep out there with all those fearsome dogs and wild animals about. While we debated the problem, two figures came panting up to us: the man and boy from the stationary lorry who had seen our headlights and had guessed our plight.

These two immediately dived into the bonnet, and, after much talking, gesticulating, blowing and switching the engine on and off, they seemed to know what was wrong. They removed part of the engine, possibly the gasket. Amid this chaotic scene a huge lorry, crowded with men, women and children, arrived and stopped beside us. The driver came and looked at our engine. He was young, quiet and confident. He worked quietly away at the engine for an hour before he made it work again. During this time the children in the lorry began to cry. Every time I heard a child cry, I pounced upon it with a Turkish delight and so kept them quiet until the car was mended. We thanked the men and spluttered away.

After a little while, the road improved. It was now nearly 11pm, we had left Ankara very early that morning, and had not stopped since lunch at Konya. Suddenly I called to Bill to stop;

he just managed to do so in time. He had not seen a stationary lorry with no rear lights. I was extremely tired, and found the greatest difficulty in keeping my eyes open. Then Bill complained that he kept falling asleep. So we decided to stop and have a short sleep before going any further. I snuggled into my duffle coat and was asleep immediately.

Suddenly I was awakened by a torch shining in my face. Hastily gathering my scattered thoughts, I remembered where I was and awakened Bill. It was just two men who were passing in a lorry, and they came to see if we were all right. We had slept for an hour, and so decided to drive on. I felt even more tired than before. I only hoped that Bill felt better, but I dared not ask him.

After a time we reached a tiny village where we had coffee and melon. There were no hotels. Men crowded round us and we must have looked a strange sight. We were coated in dust and very tired. We drove on to Eregli.

In Eregli all walls, houses and hotels were made of mud. It was midnight and the village was asleep. We stopped thankfully at the first place marked *Oteli* and before we had a chance to get out of the car, the hotel keeper and his assistant rushed out to greet us.

The night was cold and the interior of the hotel was also cold. In hotels, nothing ever seemed to happen on the ground floor, so we immediately ascended to the office on the first floor where we asked, in English and Turkish, for single bedrooms. The

Turks could not conceive of two strangers of the opposite sex travelling together and not belonging to each other. We eventually thought that they had understood, but discovered that we had been given a room with single beds. We re-explained, and Bill was given a bed in the office.

The hotel was run by two men: one old and one young. The old one was grey haired, charming and courteous, and the young one was rather the 'smart alec' type.

There was only one place for washing, and that was where the lavatories were. Having made certain that no one was there, I went in. The doors did not lock. Afterwards I decided to try to wash some of the dust off my feet in the washbasin. The old man appeared and stood by holding the towel. He seemed intrigued. He came with me to my room and brought me an earthenware pitcher of water and a glass. He then asked me if I wanted my key on the outside. I replied firmly that I would have it on the inside. I said goodnight and locked the door.

The sleeping mud village looked mysterious by moonlight as I looked out from my bedroom window. Being cold and a little hungry, I climbed into a clean bed, where the top sheet was safety-pinned onto a quilt – there were no blankets.

Next morning I awakened and dressed at 5am and, on going to the office, found Bill sleeping soundly. Since the early start was his idea, I awakened him and then went for a stroll while he dressed.

The whole place was wide awake and bathed in early morning

sun. It was market day, and the main square was full of sheep; there were also goats and donkeys. The mud houses were quaint and small, and built along the narrow, winding earth roads. I made my way with difficulty through the animals and men and, because the air was still cold, I soon returned to the hotel.

In the hotel I met an old, poorly dressed peasant woman, who looked cold and was eating a ring of bread. These rings were about the size of the palm of one's hand with no centre. They were dry and had sesame seeds stuck on top. They were the only thing to be bought in the early morning. The old woman broke a piece off her bread ring and gave it to me. She seemed so sincerely delighted to meet me that I could not hurt her feelings by offering her money, and I felt badly about eating her breakfast. We had no common language, but somehow we understood each other.

Bill was now dressed so we paid our bills. He had to pay two shillings and six pence, and, because my room had two beds in it, I had to pay five shillings. The older man insisted that we had a glass of tea with him, and then we went to the car only to discover that the back right tyre had a puncture. I was so relieved that it had not happened last night, or it would have been the last straw.

Bill tried to raise the car with a very inadequate jack that fitted through a hole by the driver's seat. The back was heavily laden down with all Bill's luggage, and the car would not rise sufficiently to get the wheel off. We found a block of wood and managed to wedge this under the back of the car, and, after much stress and strain, and assistance from the locals, Bill managed to change the wheel and we went on our way rejoicing. It was another beautiful day with a brilliant sun rising into a clear, blue sky.

Terry Mallory had told me that at Ulukisla there were hot springs, and that baths had been built which were famous in Turkey and were worth seeing. Since Ulukisla was on our way we decided to get there by mid-day.

The day was hot and the road dusty and bumpy, so it was not possible to go at any reasonable speed. This slowness did at least enable me to drink in the constantly changing panorama of rolling desert mountains with their varying colours. We saw camels, vultures, storks, hawks and buzzards. I had never seen a vulture before and at first thought it was an eagle. They were large brown birds with bald heads and horrible expressions. Bill recounted to me gruesome tales of vultures he had seen in India and then, on seeing a donkey, went on to expound to me the evolution of the cloven hoof.

EIGHT

Ulukisla

We reached Ulukisla before midday. There was a railway station with a train waiting at the station, and all around were people in bright, striped, hand-woven clothes with donkeys or bundles or both. There was a hotel and three restaurants. Beside the hotel, about half a dozen old men and women were squatting on the ground disembowelling and skinning sheep.

We chose the cleanest looking restaurant, and went straight to a corner of the room where the food was being prepared and pointed to what we wanted. We had an excellent meal of meat on skewers, tomatoes, egg plant, peppers and lettuce leaves. This was our first meal since lunch in Konya the day before, and we were glad of it.

The baths were up a hill opposite, and it was possible to get there by car. The road was stony, steep and winding but after only a very short drive we came upon a most colourful scene.

Tucked into the hill, along the road that now wound down and round, were long low huts. Some of these sold refreshments, others were hotels. But all around were large families or groups of people bivouacking, and everywhere was a blaze of colour from clothes and material that had been hung or laid on the ground to dry. The women here did not wear the strange Turkish trousers, but instead wore long colourful cotton dresses. I tried to discover why the change of clothing, and was told that they always wore a dress for bathing (hence the Turkish bath robe).

There were no other visitors and the greatest interest was taken in us. Nearly everyone else was resting. We bought a bath ticket and walked through the colourful mass until we came to a building much larger than the others. This was the bath house. We walked down a stone passage and were shown into cubicles. In each cubicle was one chair and a small strip of concrete floor to stand on. The rest of the floor space was the bath. It was sunk into the ground, made of concrete and there were concrete steps leading down into it. There were no taps. The place was full of steam and the water was so hot that I could not put my hand in it. Bill's bath was not so hot and very gently he managed to get in. I just bathed my feet.

Bill asked me to take a photograph of him in his bath. He wanted it for the *Daily Mail* in London. I protested that he must be decent. He was in the bath with just his head and shoulders showing. I opened the door, rushed in and snapped the camera, and rushed out again. The steam was so thick I could not see Bill. I only hope it produced something.

The hot spring that is used for these baths comes rushing down the mountains right beside the bath house where some of the water had been diverted. Steam rose from the stream, and it is in this hot stream that all the people wash their clothes. It seemed as if they had come from far and wide and, having used every change of raiment, they had come to wash the lot, and this meant the whole family moving to this spot for a time. It probably only happens a few times a year.

When I was wandering by myself, I was surrounded by women all wanting to talk to me. This was the first time that I had been mobbed by women. They were all very dark, plump and pleasant. They wanted to touch me, especially the old women, as if I were not real.

There was one very beautiful girl about sixteen. She was so beautiful that it was difficult not to stare. She spoke a little French and was extremely shy. She was of medium height, beautifully proportioned, and she had natural poise and dignity. Her olive skin was smooth; her black hair was plaited and wound round her head; her black eyes were almond shaped and fringed with long black lashes; her mouth was sensitive and her neck and features were perfect. Bill was enchanted with her, but quickly realised that she was too shy to enjoy talking to him, so he left me to talk to her. When she had nothing to say, she just sat perfectly relaxed with her hands folded lightly on her lap and gazed straight before her. I could not help feeling that here was one of the most beautiful people I had ever seen. She seemed to embody all the goodness in Eastern mysticism: calmness, serenity, repose, resignation, meditation, peace, timelessness, unselfconsciousness and unquestioning belief.

Turkish children, when they are small, are enchanting and their mothers brought them up to me for them to kiss my hand. I found this extremely embarrassing but could do nothing about it since we had no common language. The women treated me as if I were a lucky charm or a good spirit. They touched me and made their children touch me. So I just sat there until Bill had finished taking all the photographs he needed. We then waved goodbye to everyone and shook hands all round, and went on our way to Adana.

In the blazing afternoon heat, we drove through the most beautiful mountains: all red and jagged against the blatant blue sky. We came to a halt at a level-crossing where a picturesque ancient Turk lived in a tiny house and operated the level-crossing. He gave me two red apples, and the driver of a lorry gave Bill a melon.

After the train had gone, and we had finished passing the time of day with the level-crossing operator, we continued and soon found ourselves passing between the magnificent Cilician Gates. The rocky mountains almost closed in above us, and we felt very small as we continued down the gap in the shadows with never ending amazement at the magnificence of the mountains on either side.

NINE

Tarsus to Adana to Ceyhan

We diverted from our route slightly and went to Tarsus because St. Paul was my favourite Saint. Tarsus was disappointing. Hot and smelly with small new houses, much poverty, and a few noisy motorcars overflowing with very dark, vulgar, young Turks, hooting loudly and leering. We stopped for coffee which we drank in a tree-shaded courtyard beside the main road, where there was a handsome young cockerel perched on the back of a chair at our table.

The only part of old Tarsus that remained was a remnant of the city walls and the Western Gate. It was massive and typically Roman. Within the wall beside the gate was a small and dark forge. This was the only attractive part of the town.

We soon left Tarsus, and drove eastwards towards Adana. Adana was very full and since it was only early evening, we decided to drive on. Bill offered to take me either to Osmaniyz in the mountains, or to Payas by the sea.

Suddenly the sun began to set and since it was so beautiful

and we were driving west, we stopped at a roadside café to have coffee and watch until it almost disappeared. One of the customers in the café insisted on paying for us and they all surrounded the car and waved us 'goodbye'. After some time, we reached Misis where we stopped and stood on the bridge over a river to watch the end of the sunset. There being no hotel in Misis, we drove on to Ceyhan and, because it was now dark, we decided to stay there for the night.

The hotel was modern, ugly and hot. We both decided to have a hot bath, but the bath was full of dirty water and the plug hole was stopped up. However, the bath was eventually emptied and joyfully I went into the bathroom, only to discover that the hot tap would do no more than trickle, so I bathed in the trickle and dressed for dinner. We went to a typical food shop and ate a huge meal and many slices of melon.

Bill wanted to go to a Turkish cinema, so off we went. The cinema manager insisted on giving us free seats, and we were ushered into an open air cinema where very fat Turks had to move up to make room for us. The film, about a woman, her husband, and her lover, was violent. Her husband's friend threatened to tell her husband so she stabbed him with a pair of scissors. Her lover put the body in a cart and tipped it into the river. Later, when she had run away with her lover and was living happily, the husband unexpectedly met the lover, they had a fight, the lover was killed and the husband strapped the dead lover over his horse which made its own way back to the woman in the sunset with vultures circling overhead. I found it horrible and frightening, as did Bill, but the Turkish audience was unmoved. We decided never to visit a Turkish cinema again.

Very tired, we went back to the hotel.

Next morning we had coffee and discovered which bus would take me on to Maras. This was where our ways parted and I was sorry to lose Bill's very congenial company. The bus left Ceyhan, and I was alone on my way to Hittite country armed only with the few Turkish words Terry Malloy had given me: 'toilet; where?; lunchroom; yes; no; bus; I want to see; ancient arts; can I go there?; English teacher'.

The bus was full and all were men except for one heavily veiled and escorted woman. The bus left the low ground and climbed gradually to quite hilly country. We stopped halfway and had coffee, then went on to Maras. We reached there at 2pm, the driver carried my bag to a hotel, and gave me in charge to the hotel keeper. One other passenger also came to the hotel. He was a school teacher who could speak no English, French or German.

An unpleasant hotel manager took my passport, and escorted me upstairs to a fair-sized room like a prison.

Very hot, tired and with a splitting headache, I rested for an hour. My room was on the first floor and had no windows. It had a wash hand basin but no other facilities. The bed linen was disgusting and the room hot and airless. By 3pm I felt considerably refreshed, so left my room to discover that the school teacher had been sitting outside my room the whole time, waiting to escort me on a tour of Maras. Since we could speak no word of a common language, he had collected a student who spoke a few words of English, and the three of us sallied forth into the blazing afternoon sun.

TEN

Maras

Maras looked attractive in the sun. High in the bare mountains of central Turkey it had only a main street, a few side streets and an ancient covered market.

The old market was fascinating. It was a warren of dimly lit old stone subways with brightly coloured fruit and clothes displayed on either side. It was crowded with people, many of whom were deformed or diseased with leprosy.

After leaving the market I walked down the main street, and was joined by some young men who were students, wanting to practice their English. Soon I had about twenty escorts, when suddenly a breathless youth with black, curly hair, rushed up to me, shook me firmly by the hand and said:

'Welcome to Maras. I heard a stranger had arrived. My parents would be honoured if you would eat with us tonight.'

I thanked him and said that I should be delighted.

He spoke English fluently and abounded with energy. He told me how his father was very rich and how he was studying to become a doctor of medicine, and that his father was going to send him to a university in America; that he had an older brother and sister, and that his sister and mother would be interested to see what I was wearing.

We scrambled down the hill and visited a mosque. I said that I should like to climb the minaret and stand where the muezzin stands when he calls the people to prayer. Sitting in the courtyard were some old men who said that it was unsafe for me to go up because I should fall off the tower. The door to the tower was locked but some students rushed off and returned with the key.

It was pitch black inside and the stairs wound steeply round and up, and the minaret was so narrow that I only just fitted. This, coupled with the darkness and the fact of having unknown students before and behind gave me a feeling of claustrophobia and insecurity and, as I climbed higher, I became slightly breathless and dizzy. Just as I began to think that I should never reach the top, I saw a small shaft of light and soon reached a small hole. I doubled myself up and crawled through onto a narrow balcony with a low wall. We were now at the top of the minaret, and the courtyard seemed very far below. Going down was not so bad.

My student friends suggested that we had a drink in the park. It was extremely hot, so we sat outside, I on a chair and the boys on the grass, drinking tea or coffee. The park was full of men resting, and slowly these men moved near us until they were all sitting on the grass row upon row in a semi-circle facing me. They just sat silently, gazing. Then one of the students explained that no woman ever visited the park. I realised then that I had seen few women in Maras, and those few had their faces heavily veiled.

The student who had invited me to dine at his home was called Orhan, and he thought it time for us to go, so I said farewell to my escort of students and we set off to Orhan's house. We were met in the street by his elder brother, a tall, dark, handsome man and his nephew, Marmet. Marmet was five years old and the most enchanting little boy I had ever seen. He was very brown and beautifully made with black almond shaped eyes and a heavenly smile. He was Orhan's sister's child and was quite unspoilt.

The house where Orhan lived was a large, modern, western type house with a garden in front. At the side of the house they had a cow chained, just as we might have a dog, in order to have milk on the spot. Inside, the house was spacious and well designed, all the floors were of highly polished light brown wood, and on the walls of the rooms hung lovely, bright carpets. The furniture was modern and in good taste. As in most hot countries, they lived on the first floor, using the ground floor for the kitchens. Leading off the rooms on the first floor was a wide, wooden, covered balcony with trailing plants.

Orhan's mother and sister were both short, round, dark and charming. They couldn't speak English, but we all sat down and talked with Orphan acting as interpreter, while Marmet sat on the sofa cracking nuts with his teeth and throwing the shells on the floor. A little servant girl, about twelve years old, immediately darted across the room and picked the broken shells off the carpet.

Orphan then said that he would like to show me his English library. To my astonishment I discovered that his English library consisted only of a magazine of pin-ups of Marilyn Monroe. I said with surprise: 'Marilyn Monroe!'

Orhan said eagerly, 'How you say her? I always want to know how you say her. Please teach me.'

So, with the family nodding approval that their son should improve his English, I solemnly taught him those two magic words: Marilyn Monroe.

One of the servant girls then came with a metal bowl of water in which I rinsed my hands. We sat down at a small table on the balcony to our evening meal. Only the men sat down with me: Orhan, his brother, a cousin and Marmet. His mother disappeared and his sister waited on us charmingly.

We had a wonderful meal, with lots of courses during which Marmet's father arrived and joined us. He was tall and fair with blue eyes, most unusual in Anatolia. He couldn't speak English. Then Orhan's father arrived.

Marmet shouted, 'Look who's here!' pointing at me and jumping up and down.

We all stood and solemnly I was presented. I felt that this

man was important, and that this was an occasion. He was a fine, noble type of man: very tall, well built, dark, with black eyes and black hair. He did not eat with us but sat talking while we ate. He couldn't speak English so Orhan interpreted and his opening remark to me was, 'To which political party in England do you belong?'

'I don't take an active part in politics,' I replied.

He next asked where I came from and what I did. Having satisfied himself on those points, he left us. I felt that he was a strangely cold man; neither friendly nor hostile, just completely unemotional.

Orhan's sister asked if I would stay with them and showed me the guest room. It was delightful, with bright, clean chintzes and carpets and a telephone beside the bed. It was the height of comfort, and without a moment's hesitation, I accepted their kind invitation and thought of not having to sleep in the filthy, windowless hotel bedroom with great relief. So, leaving my camera, sunglasses and dictionary, Orhan, his brother and cousin took me by car to the hotel to collect my luggage. Because I was in the taxi, the light had to be on. This was the law if a woman was a passenger.

Oran explained that his father had an aeroplane and we would fly to their farm in the south. This sounded most exciting. It was about 9pm when we reached the hotel, and I ran upstairs to collect my bag. On coming down, I was met by a very troubled Orhan, who said that the hotel manager would not let me leave the hotel on orders from the chief of police. I told Orhan that I had no intention of staying one moment longer in the hotel, and I asked the hotel manager for my passport, which he had asked for on my arrival. The manager refused to give it to me. I then asked him to put through a telephone call to the British Embassy in Ankara. He would not do this either but remained absolutely stationary and silent. Orhan said he would telephone the chief of police and explain.

After a brief telephone conversation, Orhan said it was no good, the chief of police had given orders that I was not to leave the hotel. They all talked of the chief of police with bated breath.

I protested that I must return to Orhan's home to thank and say farewell to his parents and sister. Orhan explained that there was no need for thanks since what they had done was only their duty to a stranger. However, I took his address so that I could write. Then I remembered I had left my camera, sunglasses and dictionary at his home. So Orhan went back in the car for them, while his brother and cousin remained with me. When Orhan returned he had my camera and dictionary, but had forgotten my sunglasses. I couldn't ask him to go back yet again, so I thanked him and said goodbye.

I was sorry to see them depart and felt rather cut off and alone in the dismal hotel prison. There was nothing else to do but go to my windowless bedroom and lock myself in.

I was not happy about being divorced from my passport, but since there was nothing I could do about it, I decided to go to bed. I had only just undressed when there was a knock on the door.

Putting on my dressing gown, I opened the door and discovered a small, dark, young policeman standing there. He smiled and through signs made me understand that I was to remain in the hotel to sleep, and must not go to Orhan's home. I then explained, by signs, that my sunglasses were at Orhan's home and that since I could not get them, he must get them for me and leave them downstairs at the hotel office. He seemed to understand and, still smiling, departed.

I decided that it would be best for me to leave Maras next day and I knew that the only way was by bus that left at 4.30am for Malatya. So, with the intention of getting up at 4am I went to bed and fell asleep.

I was awakened about 11.30pm by the sound of men outside my door wearing heavy boots; there was also a loud knocking on the door. Having put on my dressing gown, I unlocked the door and there was the little, dark policeman with another dark policeman and two soldiers with rifles and fixed bayonets. I thought I was about to be arrested, but the policeman thrust my sunglasses at me. I murmured '*Merci*'. The two soldiers rushed towards me with astonished faces while I hastily retreated and locked the door.

They went away. I breathed a sigh of relief, said my prayers for the second time that night and went to bed again, having first pushed the bed against the door.

Far, far away there came the sound of knocking. Then suddenly I was awake, worried and confused. There was more knocking and it was on my door and it was a definite, loud, demanding knock. I looked at my watch: it was half an hour after midnight, so I decided not to open the door. The knocking continued, accompanied by shouts of '*Politzi, Politzi!*' I felt perhaps it would be wiser to open the door if it were the police, so again putting on my dressing gown, I turned the key and opened the door a little way.

Standing right up against the door was a man in a brown suit and a brown trilby hat. He was wearing a stiff, white collar, a white shirt and a brown tie with a small design. He was clean, well dressed, slim and very dark with black eyes. With him was the hotel manager.

The man in the brown suit looked at me from under the brim of his trilby hat, worn at an angle well down over the left eye, and hissed through his teeth, '*Chief Politzi*, passport'.

So this was the great chief of police of Maras. I indicated to him that the hotel manager had my passport and he sent him off to fetch it.

The chief of police remained standing there. I had difficulty in keeping my eyes open in the bright corridor light but my mind was awake and full of apprehension. My thoughts drifted to the crusades and of the terrible things that happened to Christians at the hands of the Turks. My apprehension rose. I asked him if he spoke English, French, German or Russian. But he shook his head to all, so I shrugged my shoulders and we reverted to standing there in silence; he watching me and I with a blank face gazing into space. He was standing very close, right against the door way. I was conscious of the thinness of my night attire.

The hotel manager returned with my passport which I knew to be in order. The chief of police grabbed it and shouted, '*Turkishka visa, Turkishka visa!*' tapping my passport.

'Passport *taman*,' I replied, meaning, 'passport all right'.

Then both the chief of police and the hotel manager began waving their arms about and shouting about *Turkishka visa* with an abundance of Turkish that meant nothing to me. Whenever there was a pause, I just solemnly repeated, 'Passport *taman*,' which immediately set them off again. The chief of police shouted again, '*Turkishka visa!*' He was getting most excited.

Since all my attempts to convince him that as a tourist travelling on a British passport I did not need a Turkish visa, failed, I took my passport from him and, in desperation, looked through it for inspiration.

My eye fell on the last page of the passport where the Turkish authorities on the Greek/Turkish frontier had put their entry stamp right across where the words were written 'Bearer previously travelled on Singapore passport,' giving a number and date. This was my last hope, which I grasped with both hands and, relying on the fact that he could not read English, I pointed to this and said with great confidence, '*Turkishka visa taman*'.

The chief of police looked doubtful. He inspected it, shook his head and muttered something in Turkish. I now considered it my turn to get annoyed. I opened the passport to the last page and in my turn shouted, '*Turkishka visa!*' and decided that this was the moment to close the interview.

I clasped his hand and shook it firmly saying '*Merci, merci,*' quickly pulled my hand away, and slammed the door shut and locked it.

I stood quite still behind the door in the darkness of my room, holding my breath and waiting. Nothing happened. All was silence. So for the third time that night I went to bed.

A few hours later I awakened. It was nearly 4am and time to get up. Since there were no windows in the room, I had no idea how light it was. I dressed hurriedly, put on my duffle coat, picked up my bag, and without making a sound, very carefully opened the door an inch and waited, listening. All was silent. I opened the door further. Down the corridor on the left two soldiers slept with their rifles across their knees. Sprawled across the stairs, the hotel manager lay sleeping.

Cautiously I crept out of my room. I stepped carefully over the sleeping hotel manager and saw a small room with the door open. On the table was my passport.

Holding my breath and making no noise, I crept into the room, picked up my passport and left a handful of money. Silently I continued downstairs and into the street. I stood quite still, breathing deeply. All was quiet.

It was just before dawn, the sky was grey and the air cool. I walked quickly along the road to the bus stop. There were a few people, one a soldier. He greeted me.

'Ha! Ha! A Montgomery woman!' he exclaimed, seeing my duffle coat.

I smiled at him.

'Do you know General Montgomery?' asked the soldier.

I lied. 'Yes, I know him well,' I replied.

'I look after you,' said the soldier finally.

I sat beside him in the bus. He had a chicken on his knees and fed it on large, green grapes throughout the journey. Each time the chicken swallowed a grape, it shut its eyes and looked as if it were about to choke.

ELEVEN

Malatya

The bus to Malatya was crowded but the soldier was very protective of me and his chicken. I was relieved to have left Maras and wondered if there would be repercussions.

We climbed onto a high plateau and travelled the whole way through grassless mountains. The road was not good but was serviceable, and we made good speed past a landscape that was now becoming familiar to me: mud villages, huge dogs, donkeys, camels, storks, very dark, ragged men and isolated water pumps.

We only made two halts. The little teacher was in the bus and he also looked after me. I realised again the necessity for having some man attached. We reached Malatya about mid-day.

Malatya was quite a large prosperous town, with vast white buildings and good tarmac roads. I bade farewell to the soldier. The school teacher took me to a quite clean hotel run by a very old man. It was hot so I rested in my room until 3pm. When I came out I found the school teacher waiting for me.

With great difficulty, he made me understand that he wanted

185

to show me something. He had two other young men with him. We walked down the shady side of a main street which had large, white, square residential houses on either side.

We climbed to the top floor of one of these by an outside iron stairway and arrived on a balcony. The school teacher knocked on a door. After some delay this was opened by a girl of about twenty-two years. They spoke for a moment in Turkish, then the girl turned to me and in perfect English invited me to come in. The men went away after having asked my permission to go.

Two other girls then appeared. They were all wearing loose fitting cotton gowns rather like old fashioned nightdresses: high at the neck and with long sleeves. They explained that they had been bathing.

One of the girls made the most delicious Turkish coffee which we all drank. These Turkish girls were teachers of English and their home was in Smyrna. They lived together in this tiny flat and were rather lovely.

The girls then dressed in pretty cotton frocks and said they would show me Malatya, and we would have dinner in the Officers Club.

Mayatya seemed a fairly civilised place and I was not molested in any way. The shops were small and the clothes were dull. Most of the women had their faces covered and did not look as if they approved of our Western undress.

The girls told me that it is the men, i.e. the husbands, who like their women covered, and that many women, particularly if they know they are attractive, will uncover their face when they see a man, so long as their husband is not around.

After a time we left the main street and went up a narrow mud and stone lane. The houses now became shacks and there was evidence of great poverty. The lane petered out and we followed a grass path up a hill side.

A new road was being made, and we had difficulty in climbing over newly thrown up red clay. The wind was quite strong and the evening cool as we climbed the hill.

From the top, we saw the most lovely view of Malatya nestling in among the hills. The sun was setting and the lights from the town began to twinkle as we came down the hill and made our way to the Officers Club.

This was not as large as the one in Konya, and was much more Eastern. Some officers were with their wives, and the school teachers introduced me to their friends. We had a great deal of food put before us, and I explained that I was on my way to Bogazkoy.

They tried to persuade me to stay in Malatya and to go to their museum where there was much about the Hittite kingdom. They did not understand the excitement of digging and discovering.

The bus left early for Sivas next morning so I decided to catch it.

TWELVE

Sivas

The bus left the mountainous country around Malatya and descended to the usual arid desert, often with a light vegetation. We came across small rivers and drove straight through them at speed.

All the passengers were men. Their skin was dark and weathered. They were slim, muscular, of medium height. Most wore cloth caps and often carried rough sticks. They neither smiled at me nor spoke to me, but just looked.

It was cool in the early morning, so I wore a navy blue cardigan. Suddenly I felt pinches, on my behind where there was a gap between the back of the seat and the seat itself. I tried to ignore this. Then pinches came from both sides as my arms, shoulders and chest were pinched.

Everywhere was so dusty that I was now covered with dusty pinch marks all over my dark, wool cardigan. I reached for my duffle coat in order to wear it as a protection. There was a murmuring that became louder. I thought the men were going to start fighting.

The driver stopped the bus. He told me to get out and to climb in with him. He spoke sternly to the men and there was silence. I was apprehensive. We were in a desert and all the passengers were very much 'elemental man'. There was just the little bus driver to keep order and things were getting out of hand.

The bus was small, old and uncomfortable with hard seats. The wheels were large, which meant that I had to climb high up into the driver's seat which was meant for one person.

The driver, being small, made it possible for me to squeeze in beside him, but there were the gears that made it most uncomfortable. My legs were in a confined space with his legs, and I had to keep my sandaled feet from being damaged as he crashed his boots onto the pedals.

The sun was blazing down on the driver's little glass cabin, and the engine gave extra heat. I accepted that there was no alternative.

About midday we came across a shepherd with a few sheep. The bus stopped. This was obviously the lunch stop. The shepherd grabbed a sheep, cut its throat, disembowelled and skinned it. This was completed in the blink of an eye. The driver had made me sit between the shepherd and himself, so I had a grandstand view.

The men sat around on the ground, talking quietly. The shepherd cut the meat into pieces, and cooked them over red hot embers. The driver had a bag of bread. The shepherd put pieces of cooked meat on chunks of bread and handed them round. It was excellent.

Everyone gave the shepherd money, but the driver would not

allow me to contribute. We resumed our journey to Sivas, which we reached mid-afternoon.

Sivas was large and built on the mountain side; the bus stopped at the bottom. The town was a mixture of modern and ancient buildings. There was a most attractive bridge over the River Kizil and there were many old buildings which were large and impressive, built in the old Turkish style.

I took photographs of the bridge and many other parts of the town as I climbed up the mountain side to a hotel the bus driver had recommended.

The hotel was most attractively built, looking down on the town. It had many balconies with flowering plants trailing everywhere. The manager was delightful and showed me into a charming room.

I bathed, changed my clothes, and went in search of a long drink. I sat in a large, comfortable chair on a balcony surrounded by flowering plants, idly gazing down on the town below and the distant mountains.

After the events in Maras and the difficult journey, this seemed like another world. All was quiet, cool and serene. I had my camera with me and was considering taking scenic photographs.

My peace was suddenly disturbed by the entrance of a young man who bounced up to me and told me he was a German student, and had just come out of prison where he had been kept because he had taken photographs of parts of the town that are listed as being in the Defence Area. These were similar to the ones I had just taken myself.

He seemed pleased to have found someone to talk to. He was about seventeen, of medium height, stockily built and blond. His English was fluent. He pulled up his shirt and showed me a two inch belt he was wearing. He had not been stripped in prison so still had it. It was of solid silver, attractively wrought with flowers and animals. He was taking it home for his sister.

Just then he threw his camera into my lap and ran from the room. I saw two policemen approaching from another direction. Quickly I sat on both the cameras, pulled out my skirt and looked at the view.

The two policemen came and stood in front of me. I smiled at them. They spoke English and asked for my passport. They studied it and then questioned me, asking where I had come from. I did not mention Maras but said Konya. Why was I in Turkey, where was I going, etc?

To my relief, they returned my passport. I continued to smile and explained that I was a traveller who liked to visit countries I did not know. I was on my way back to Istanbul and England. That I enjoyed their countryside and climate. I told them about the British climate.

They made copious notes and departed. The German student returned. I gave him back his camera and he explained that he was leaving Sivas. I was thankful because he spelt trouble. I felt the situation was precarious enough without the additional complication of an aggressive young German.

THIRTEEN

Kayseri

Clad in my duffle coat to protect me from the attentions of the other passengers, I set off for Kayseri in the local bus which left at dawn. It was quite cold but I knew once the sun was up, it would be sweltering.

As the sky changed from dawn to early morning with soft orange, pink and yellow strips melding into each other, one felt lonely and insignificant. Then, as the sun slowly peeped above the horizon, the world became a more friendly place.

The road ran beneath the mountains, following the River Kizilm, which wound south west to Kayseri, before turning north to flow into the Black Sea at Bafra Burun.

My one thought now was to get to Bogazkoy. This was caused partly because having a meal had proved almost impossible, and I had lost almost a stone in weight. I also hoped to find a European who could join me for a meal.

Hotels did not provide food so one went to a restaurant. These were quite small and primitive, wooden tables and chairs on a rough wooden floor. Not a woman in sight. The food never changed. The only trouble was that I was never able to eat any.

I would choose a table, sit down and never look directly at anyone. The men would sit on the chairs and gradually shuffle their chairs in a circle around me. Their dark eyes, unblinking, never left my face. Slowly, as if by common consent, they shuffled their chairs nearer and nearer. There was no haste, no one spoke. The waiter would come and I would order food and drink.

The men were all peasants, lean and virile, wearing Turkish peasant clothes often with black, flat caps. Many were handsome in a rough way. As the circle of chairs got nearer, the atmosphere became tense. The food had not arrived.

When they were in a circle about a foot away, I would quickly get up and walk out of the building, careful not to run. I would go back to my hotel and not leave. This had happened ever since I left Maras, whenever I attempted to eat in a restaurant.

I decided it was too dangerous and better just to drink water in the hotel.

FOURTEEN

Bogazkoy

The manager of the hotel in Kayseri was helpful when I explained that I wanted to go to Bogazkoy. He promised to find transport for me to go there next morning.

He was as good as his word and, waiting for me outside the hotel, was an old jeep with four rather noisy men. The hotel manager discussed the cost of the journey with them so I knew what to give them.

They had left the front seat for me, so amid shouts and laughter we set off. Fortunately, two of the men could speak some English. I explained my interest in the Hittites and they assured me that Hittites were everywhere, waving their arms around expansively.

There was no road between Kayseri and Bogazkoy, so we drove cross country into the golden desert, bumping and lurching, always accompanied by much laughter and the men shouting to each other above the noise of the vehicle.

We headed due north. As the crow flew the journey would be

thirty-one miles. We soon reached Erkilet, a tiny desert town, and drove on over the ridge to flat land. Next we crossed the River Kizil. There were no bridges, so we drove fast through the water.

Some distance from the river was another desert range of high sand dunes. The driver drove along the ridge until he found a convenient way through.

We were now on a desert plateau. It was exceedingly hot and we came across a well. This was a hole in the ground. Lying beside the well was a small tin can with a long piece of string attached through a small hole in the side of the tin.

The driver stopped. We all climbed out. One of the men let the can down into the well. It was fairly deep. Then they pulled it up and handed it round. We each had a small drink and passed it on. It was let down about three times. I noticed the can was a little rusty, but the water tasted clean and was very welcome. We then drove merrily on, bumping along on the hard seats.

Soon we stopped again. One of the men exclaimed 'Hittites'! He picked up a piece of stone the size of a small square headstone and gave it to me. I thanked them but explained that I was quite unable to carry it; it was too heavy and I was travelling by buses or trains.

I was loath to leave it behind. It was covered with hieroglyphics. They then gave me other small pieces which I accepted and dropped into my bag.

The desert had been whipped into hard ridges by the wind, and, looking ahead, we saw Bogazkoy rising up about three hundred metres from the desert with large heaps of rocks everywhere. There seemed to be a broken wall around the city, so we drove through a gap and then stopped.

I went up to a group of people who explained that they were French archaeologists. They took me on a tour of the ancient capital.

In the wall which surrounded the city was a large arch and five gates. At the highest point was a gate with the head of sphinxes and two other gates, the Royal gates, had a lion. There were large statues made of stone.

The city centre seemed to be mostly temples which were being reconstructed, but there was still much to be discovered. The streets were made of large flat stones. Everywhere there were large, heavy stones. The solidity of the place was imposing. It was an exciting moment to stand in the great Hittite capital that was first inhabited in the third millennium B.C., with all its subsequent history. There was a citadel, temples and fortifications as monuments to the past, and much more to be found, but because I had no experience of digging or of this period of archaeology, they were not prepared to let me join them. This was most disappointing. They were unfriendly. Finally I signed and wrote in the visitors' book.

I gazed around at this ancient city being re-discovered, isolated in the golden desert. Sadly, I went down the many steps and back to the jeep. I gazed back at Bogazkoy until it melted into the evening mist where the desert meets the horizon.

Mike met me at Ankara. I was dirty, tired and hungry. I had lost weight and Mike did not recognise me. I explained how impossible it was to have a meal or a shower.

There was an urgent message for me to return to Trieste immediately where an important political announcement was to be made.

So after a shower, and a meal, I went immediately to Istanbul to catch the Orient Express for Trieste, my Anatolian journey over, but the experience imprinted for ever on my memory.

Fortunately I could quickly recover from my latest exploits with a hot bath and a good night's sleep in Istanbul, and with the feeling of relief at being safe and secure I would be quite revived.

There really was an emergency. The administration of Trieste was to be handed over to the Italians immediately and therefore The Free State of Trieste was to be disbanded. So with that news we had to get out of the area within a short set of days.

Early the next morning I caught the Simplon Orient Express back to Trieste. It really was the only train to travel on – so romantic and glamourous and with everyone so beautifully dressed. As the train swept through the landscape and I was concentrating on just how to evacuate the team, I was approached by a charming French man who offered me coffee in his cabin. He was so gallant that I found myself accepting. Later, as the train approached Trieste, he said I should come to Paris with him as he wanted to be with me. I replied somewhat tersely that I couldn't, as I had an unavoidable appointment to keep, and with that we parted.

Once packed and ready to go, with my time in Trieste at an end, I returned to London by train once again. Only this time I was sitting decorously on a box full of top secret documents and some revolvers, which you were not allowed to bring into England.

My chief clerk was a warrant officer in the Army and I asked him to sign for the box and to take it over. He said he would dispose of it safely. With that arranged I continued on towards London, still clutching the vase of flowers resting on my lap. They had been thrust into my hand by way of farewell from the Excelsior hotel.

For three years I had lived in the penthouse suite of the biggest hotel in Trieste. There were stunning and everchanging views from each of the windows of my rooms, out over the glorious Adriatic. This era of my life was over.

Once back in Whitehall I remember going to the officers' mess; a male officer came up to me and said, 'Hello, Major, have you just arrived? How are you?' I replied that I was in love, and bereft. His response was to guide me to the bar saying that what I needed was a brandy. This was the Army's solution to all problems. A drink at the bar.

I vaguely wondered if I would live to regret my somewhat sharp and firm rejection to the extraordinary yet rather wonderful proposal from the French man on the train to Trieste.

THE AUTHOR

Muriel Bol was educated at the City of London School for Girls until abruptly having to leave at the age of thirteen, to her lasting regret. She briefly attended the Bromley School of Art and the London College of Music. Her first job was with the Ministry of Labour in 1939, where she later survived a direct hit by a bomb onto the Ministry building. By 1942 she had been conscripted into the Army and found herself firing anti-aircraft guns.

After the war, the War Office sent her to Romania for the Military Intelligence. Stalinist Romania left a lasting impression on her; to this day she still supports aid to the peoples she came to know. Work in Singapore and travels to Lapland followed, until she was assigned to Trieste for three years as head of a counter espionage team. Postings to Cyprus and Germany later continued her career.

She met and married a Dutch man in Germany where they lived for fifteen years until his retirement, at which point they moved to Norfolk. Her novel *The Poisoned Spy*, published in 1994, was set in Trieste in 1949. It portrays the world of Cold War espionage and counter espionage which she knew so well. Muriel now resides on the border of Norfolk and Suffolk.